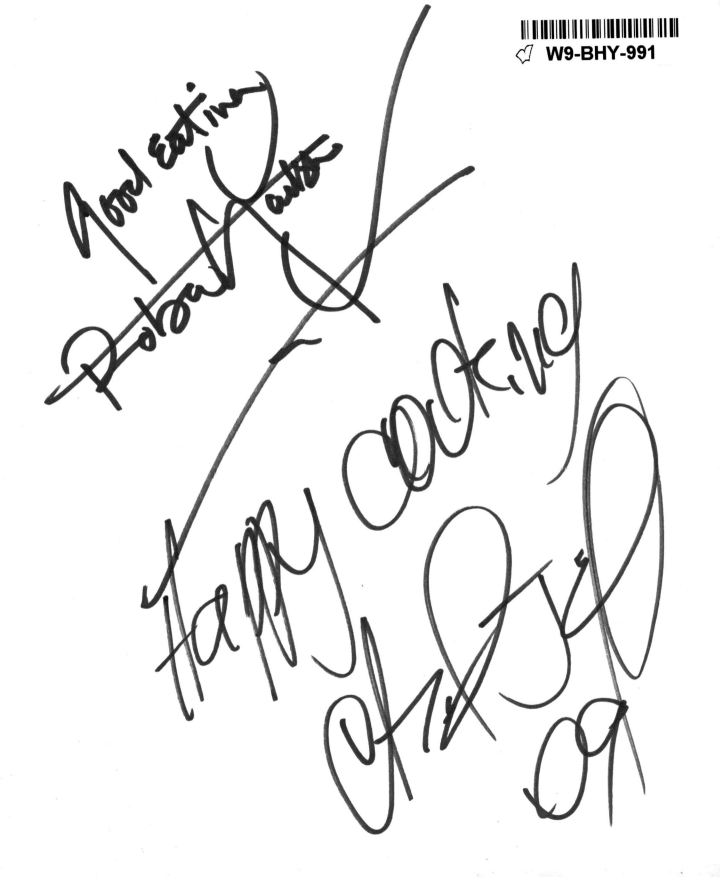

CHEF JEFF COOKS

In the Kitchen with America's
Inspirational New Culinary Star

JEFF HENDERSON

SCRIBNER

New York   London   Toronto   Sydney

SCRIBNER
A Division of Simon & Schuster, Inc.
1230 Avenue of the Americas
New York, NY 10020

First Scribner hardcover edition October 2008

SCRIBNER and design are registered trademarks of
The Gale Group, Inc., used under license
by Simon & Schuster, Inc., the publisher of this work.

For information about special discounts for bulk purchases,
please contact Simon & Schuster Special Sales:
1-800-456-6798 or business@simonandschuster.com

Designed by Kyoko Watanabe
Text set in Sabon

Manufactured in the United States of America

1 3 5 7 9 10 8 6 4 2

Library of Congress Control Number: 2008026341

ISBN-13: 978-1-4165-7710-2
ISBN-10: 1-4165-7710-6

To my granddaddy, Charles Henderson Sr., who taught my father and me to work hard and take care of business. I watched him closely in everything he did from washing store windows to manning the family stove. He never wrote down a recipe in his life, and in 1997 when I asked him for his raisin-bread pudding recipe because my wife, Stacy, was craving it during her pregnancy, he told me, "Boy, I don't have no recipe. It's in my head. You have to just get in the kitchen and watch me." He always called me *boy* in a good way. Love you, Granddaddy.

To Friendly Womack Jr., the man who taught me valuable kitchen skills when we had our little chicken business. Your willingness to teach me changed my life forever. Those basic skills have brought me into kitchens all over America and helped me inspire a new generation to learn to cook. I love you, Uncle June.

My food is a
reflection of my past.

Acknowledgments

My core team for my first cookbook has been my family, and I can't thank them enough for their unwavering support. When I search for one word to describe my wife, Stacy, my sons, Jeffery Jr. and Jamar, my two beautiful daughters, Noel Marie and Troy Kennedy, I come up with *extraordinary*! Stacy, without your patience and sacrifice, my success would have been impossible. You truly made it possible for me to translate my restaurant skills into recipes the home cook can relate to. Jeffery, Noel, and Troy, thanks for being quiet and giving up cartoons while Daddy was in the kitchen cooking, testing, and documenting recipes. Troy, you were amazing standing on a stepladder to stir the greens while Daddy worked the dough for the dinner rolls. I think you have the cooking bug. And Jamar, you ate just like Daddy: You ate it all!

Chef Robert, thanks for consulting with me on my vision for my recipes and for your continued inspiration. My literary agent, Mike Psaltis of the Culinary Cooperative, came through once again on this deal. Thanks, Mike. Beth Wareham, my editor at Scribner, the tough gal from Texas, fought hard for this project. Thanks for betting on me. Phil Davis, my lawyer, has really helped Stacy and me hold it all together. Thanks, Phil, for your integrity and for taking a special interest in my family. Betsy Pochoda, thank you for your help and for adding great vision to the stories that made this book inspiring. Chris Baker, photographer, you really showcased my passion for food through your pictures. Kudos to food stylist Lora Zarubin and to the young cook who helped me make these recipes camera ready.

To all the kitchen workers in the West from Los Angeles to San Diego to Las Vegas who have been on the front lines with me from the beginning of my professional career. Juan Carlos, Mario, and Feliciano in California helped me polish my skills enough to become a chef. My crew at Caesars Palace, Timmy and Drew, you always had my back during the rough times on my road to success.

I really want to thank the entire kitchen and stewarding crew at Café Bellagio, who gave

100 percent every day, especially during the busy season when you all stepped up to the plate. Simon Youl, the hardest-working man in the kitchen, you are a legend for keeping the kitchen organized, and your humor during service kept us all laughing. The breakfast crew, pantry ladies, and the prep crew in the back, I commend you all for the years of hard work. To the sous chefs at the café, Jamie, Kelly, Matt, Larry, and Patrick, we always made it happen when we were short and you all gave me 100 percent no matter what. Thanks.

Tammy Baker, Andrea Foggy-Paxton, and Tavis Smiley, thanks for giving me a shot at showcasing my talent for my first celebrity party. That opportunity gave me the confidence to go out and cook across America. Derek Folk, Tami Womack, Greg Evans, and Levi Jones, you all were believers from the start, and your support opened doors for me and kept me off the streets. Thank you all. La Cresha, thanks for your help on this book and for many adventures. You are very special to Stacy and me, and your input and passion for community has been invaluable.

To all my former chefs—Friendly Womack, Big Roy, Robert Gadsby, Sterling Burpee, Sara Bowman, James Perlio, Wolfgang Von Weiser, and Edmond Wong—who gave me the skills and the opportunity to feed my family, I will never forget the impact you have had on my life. To Las Vegas executives Greg Waldren, Win Person, and Bart Mahonny, thank you for signing off on my opportunities.

I want to thank all the staff at the Bellagio who helped me succeed inside and outside the company: the bartenders Pops and Gin; Tim and Martin Herling, who campaigned to get me hired; Larry, the shoeshine man who kept my clogs looking good—thanks a million to you all. Terry Lanni, thank you for taking my meetings to discuss life. You are an inspiration to many.

To Robin Carter, the Tutto manager who oversaw my best book signing, thanks for your help. To MGM/MIRAGE, I am grateful for your professionalism and support of my life story. To all the nonprofit organizations and companies that have believed in my mission: MFHA, NSMH, ARAMARK, Smithfield Foods Inc., Patterson Partners, Pro Start, C-CAP, Chicago Public Schools, Books for Boys, New York City Public Schools, Las Vegas Public Schools, Los Angeles Unified School District, and Job Corps. Bob Tushman, Brian Lando, and the Food Network, thank you for the opportunity to live my dream.

To all the young people out there, especially the ones who have fallen by the wayside, it is you whom I strive to inspire in my daily life. I draw my strength from you in all my work. Find your purpose, and your dream will come to light. Cooking is a joy for those who have a passion for pleasing. Cook hard and remember that those who sacrifice are those who win.

Contents

Introduction by Chef Jeff

Twenty years ago, I did not know what a reduction was or even how a sauté pan worked. I couldn't pronounce *foie gras,* and I certainly couldn't imagine that one day I'd know how to cook it to perfection. I'd never heard of heirloom tomatoes, now a staple on my dinner table during the summer. I never knew about slow-braising collard greens and couldn't imagine that cooking them with smoked turkey and low-sodium chicken broth would create a healthier version than the one I'd grown up on. In fact, outside of eating, I didn't give much thought to food at all. I didn't know the power of food back then, or how, twenty years later, it would change my life.

It was February 2007, just weeks before my first book, *Cooked,* would be released, and I was getting anxious about how much my life would change. I began stealing moments at work just to stand alone in the walk-in refrigerator and think. I was thinking about how, in just a few weeks' time, I would be a guest on the *Oprah Winfrey Show.* It's often said that if Oprah simply says your name, your life will change. Not only would she say my name but she also would interview me in front of millions of people. What would she ask me? How would I respond? As I think back, my appearance on her show was the beginning of a series of blessings that continue to be showered upon me and my family today.

But let me back up a little and tell you how I got to this overwhelming moment of standing alone in a walk-in refrigerator and feeling blessed but also redeemed. My road to redemption began while I was serving time in a federal prison. I was very young back then and unaware of my full potential. I was intelligent. On the streets I'd been a successful hustler, and you can't be successful in that game without smarts. In prison I developed a hunger for knowledge and began to seek and ultimately find my true purpose in life. In the end, I became a person who could use knowledge to turn his intelligence to positive ends.

Today I can look back and say that doing time was a blessing in disguise. It took me off the streets, and it led me to my destiny, cooking. I found peace in the prison kitchen. I learned who I was there. And I learned how to learn. I found myself drawn to the brightest minds on the inside, and I began to care about what was going on in the world outside. I read my first book and my first newspaper in prison, and I began to realize that I was worthy of all the good things that life had to offer. Prison put me on the road to redemption, and cooking in prison became my salvation.

I continued to have my little moments of reflection in the walk-in refrigerator at Café Bellagio, where I was executive chef. Many thoughts occupied my mind: How did it happen that I had become the first African American chef to run a restaurant in Las Vegas's world-renowned Bellagio Hotel? And to go back in time, why had a well-known chef named

Robert Gadsby given me my first job and why did he believe in me despite my questionable past? Why did Chef Sarah Bowman hire me, with just two years of professional experience, to help her revamp a hotel resort on Coronado Island? When I think back, I realize that they saw potential in me and that I believed in myself and in my dream.

I had dreamed of becoming a chef. I sacrificed. I submitted to a rigorous life of hard work. My "first in, last out" discipline kept me grinding, working long hours as I struggled to gain the respect of my mentors, coworkers, managers, and above all, my harshest critic, myself. I honed my skills behind the scenes at work and at home. I studied the competition, read books, researched recipes, and prepared for the time when I would emerge from the shadows of my mentors. My thirst for knowledge was so intense that I had few friends then, no hobbies outside of cooking, and every spare dime was spent on the latest tools of my trade.

And then, after a national book and media tour, appearances on major talk shows, and many great reviews of my book, I was still pacing around that walk-in. Guests were now coming to the restaurant just to experience my cuisine. The pacing helped, but it was a challenge for me to stay focused on my work. Finally I requested a leave of absence from my job. Hundreds of e-mails were flooding my inbox; parents and teachers were calling and asking me to mentor their children. Overnight, it seemed, I had become an inspiration to people all over the country. The sacrifices on the long journey to chefdom now seemed worth it.

Ever since I had started on the road to realizing my dream, I had worked most days of the week and all holidays and had never taken a sick day. I often had two jobs. Earning the title of chef required that kind of dedication. During my leave of absence, I started to spend time thinking about my personal and professional future. I was determined to be prepared for whatever life had in store for me. In my memoir, *Cooked,* I chronicled my journey from the streets to the stove, and the story pretty much ended right there. How was I to know that the next chapters of my life would play out just like a dream? I had always dreamed big and encouraged others to do the same. Now that the dream is real, I know that nothing except living it every day could have made it so. Every day I thank God for giving me the gift to use food to change not only my life but also the lives of others around me.

Food has led me to become an inspirational speaker for young people at risk across this country. Many of them come from challenging environments and have either given up on their dreams or have never dreamed at all. I try to bring hope to those who once felt hopeless and speak about the power of potential. When I talk, I lay out the Chef Jeff keys to success. This is a cookbook, so I'll just give you the short version:

- I tell these young people to search for their purpose in life and then to visualize a positive dream for themselves. I urge them to pursue that dream with everything they have.

- I explain the importance of building powerful relationships with other people if they want to open certain doors in life.

- I teach them the value of passion, drive, focus, and urgency in the pursuit of personal and professional goals.

- I stress the importance of growing and of changing the negative habits that get in the way of their dreams.

- I describe the steps they must take to educate themselves about how to make the right choices. I also stress the importance of understanding the consequences of those choices.

- I point out that you have to accept constructive criticism and be resilient in the face of setbacks if you are going to succeed.

- I let them know how important it is to listen, to be detail oriented, and to have integrity.

- Above all, I stress the importance of giving back to those who come after you whose journey may be more difficult than your own. Don't wait until your dream comes true to help others.

One of my proudest accomplishments has been to finish filming the first season of my reality show, *The Chef Jeff Project,* which airs on the Food Network. In it I teach many of these principles to young people at risk while they work with me in my catering company, Posh Urban Cuisine.

As I write this, my first cookbook, I can't help sharing my principles and reflections with you. I know this for sure: The journey that I've taken, with all its detours, obstacles, stop signs, potholes, and fender benders, was necessary to get me to where I am today. My life is very different now. Though I am still determined to bring new dreams to reality, I also understand the need for balance. My wife, Stacy, and four children, Jamar, Jeffery Jr., Noel, and Troy, keep me grounded. They are my inspiration. They also keep me busy. Each day at home, we have three menus. I eat everything but pork, my wife is a vegetarian, and my children, except for Jamar, are vegans (that's the subject for another book). As a family, we work together to prepare dinner. We shop together and embrace the differences in our diets. My wife is a great cook. We compete all the time in the kitchen over who creates the best flavor or the best presentation, and, around the holidays, we even compete for oven space. The time I spend with my family, in the kitchen and out, is precious and priceless.

My earliest memories in the kitchen are of seeing what my mother, June, brought home

from the store and watching my sister, Junell, prepare dinner. Though I am a professional chef, I come from a long line of great cooks, and I, too, consider myself a home cook first. The recipes in this book are reminiscent of my childhood. My family roots are deeply embedded in the South. It may seem like a cliché, but it's true that many memories are created in the kitchens of Southern households. I remember once traveling to New Orleans with my mother to visit my "Nanny." Back then you could not tell the economic status of a family by their meals. I know that Nanny worked hard and got paid very little, but it never stopped her from putting out a spread each time we visited. I can still smell her fried chicken, collard greens, and red beans and rice. And no trip to the Big Easy would be complete without a pot of seafood gumbo. In all my travels, I still have not had gumbo as good as Nanny and Granddaddy's. They'd say, "The secret is in the roux and them seasonings." The kitchen was a haven in those days. Happiness, love, and family bonds were cooked up there, and Nanny not only filled my stomach but also fed my soul. Nanny passed over a decade ago, but I've taken much of what I experienced during stays with her and incorporated it into my food and my life.

Today my kitchen is "family central." Life happens there. It's where I prepare my kids' favorite meals as we discuss our days, where I bond with my wife over morning coffee, and it's where I cook New Orleans–style gumbo for my parents just the way Nanny and Granddaddy did for me. I use chicken instead of pork sausage in my gumbo, but my father, Charles, gives it his seal of approval each time I make it.

I set out to bring some of my family's culinary history into this book along with the

influences of mentors, cooks, and chefs that I've encountered in my culinary journey. Although I have learned from chefs with international experience, my cooking here is straightforward American. I describe it as modern comfort food because these recipes begin with many childhood favorites that I have adapted and updated using farm-fresh ingredients wherever possible and incorporating the things I've learned as a professional chef. Most of my recipes have a story behind them, and I'm sharing some of those stories in this book. I hope, as you try my recipes, you'll begin to create your own memories and stories to go with your meals.

This is not just a cookbook; it's a testimonial to my desire to succeed and inspire lives. It's also a tribute to those who have been instrumental in shaping who I am today. I found my way into the kitchen by accident, but I believe today it was my destiny. God gave me my life's vision behind the stove, and cooking has become my gift to you.

Bon appétit,
Chef Jeff Henderson

CHEF JEFF COOKS

STOCKS AND BROTHS

Stocks and broths may not be new to you, but when I was growing up, the only stock or broth I knew about was what we called "pot liquor"—the liquid left after greens or meat had been cooked. My granddaddy and my sister saved this and used it in soups, rice and beans, and so forth.

In my first restaurant job I was amazed by the huge pots simmering away with various broths, aromatic herbs, and vegetables. The chef taught me that chicken stock is the basis for many, many elements in great cuisine. I think it is worth learning how to make your own stock because it's not hard to do and it freezes well in plastic containers or baggies. You can even freeze it as ice cubes and pop one in a soup or a braise for additional flavor. Good-quality chicken broth is available in stores; look for the brands that are lowest in sodium and fat.

Beef stock requires a little more effort to make, but it, too, is great to have on hand. All stocks peak in flavor the longer they cook, so that's something to consider when you are making your own.

Chicken Stock

Yields 2 quarts

WHAT YOU'LL NEED

Bones from 2 medium cooked chickens

2 medium carrots, washed, peeled, and cut into 1-inch pieces

1 small onion, peeled and quartered

2 medium stalks celery, washed and cut into 1-inch pieces

1 small bunch parsley, washed, stems removed

1 sprig fresh thyme

1 bay leaf

1 teaspoon whole white peppercorns

About 4 quarts water

WHAT TO DO

1. Remove the meat from the chicken carcasses, rinse the bones, and place the bones in a stockpot.

2. Add all of the remaining ingredients except the water.

3. Add water to cover by 2 inches. Bring to a boil, then reduce the heat for a low simmer, so that one or two bubbles break the surface of the stock about once a minute. Simmer, uncovered, for 2 to 3 hours, using a large spoon to skim off the foam until the stock is clear.

4. Pour the stock through a strainer into a clean bowl and allow to cool. Refrigerate, covered, for up to 3 days. Discard the hardened layer of fat on the top before using or freezing.

Chicken Broth

Yields 3 quarts

WHAT YOU'LL NEED

1 large chicken

1 medium onion, peeled and quartered

2 medium carrots, washed, peeled, and
     cut into 1-inch pieces

2 stalks celery, washed and cut into 1-inch pieces

1 leek (green tops only), washed and cut into 1-inch pieces

3 sprigs fresh thyme or 1 teaspoon dried

½ bunch flat-leaf parsley

2 bay leaves

1 teaspoon whole black peppercorns

About 4 quarts water

WHAT TO DO

1. Combine the chicken, vegetables, herbs, and peppercorns in a large stockpot. Pour in enough water to just cover the chicken completely. Bring the water to a boil over medium-high heat. Immediately reduce the heat for a low simmer, so that one or two bubbles break the surface of the broth about once a minute.

2. Skim the foam and discard impurities from the surface with a large spoon. (To prevent losing a lot of broth when skimming, put the skimmed liquid into a degreasing cup and return any usable broth to the pot.) Cook, uncovered, until the chicken is cooked through but not dry, about 1 hour.

3. Remove the chicken from the pot but continue to simmer the broth. Cool the chicken for about 30 minutes. Cut the meat from the bones and reserve for a chicken salad, soup, or other recipe. Return the bones to the pot and cook for 1 hour more.

4. Pour the broth through a strainer into a plastic container or large bowl. Use immediately, or cover and refrigerate or freeze for future use.

5. The broth can be stored, covered, in the refrigerator for up to 5 days. If the broth has not been used after 5 days, bring it to a boil again and skim the surface, discarding impurities, before using.

Turkey Stock

Yields 3 quarts

WHAT YOU'LL NEED

1 large turkey carcass

1 medium onion, peeled and quartered

2 carrots, washed, peeled, and cut into 1-inch pieces

2 stalks celery, washed and cut into 1-inch pieces

4 cloves garlic, peeled and chopped

2 bay leaves

4 sprigs fresh thyme

1 tablespoon whole black peppercorns

About 1 gallon water

Salt to taste

WHAT TO DO

1. Using a sharp knife, cut the carcass into small pieces. Add the bones, vegetables, bay leaves, thyme, and peppercorns to a large stockpot. Cover with water and bring to a boil.

2. Reduce the heat for a low simmer, so that one or two bubbles break the surface of the stock about once a minute. Simmer, uncovered, for 2 hours. Skim off the foam and discard impurities that rise to the surface. Add salt to taste, remove from the heat, and pour the stock through a strainer into a plastic container or large bowl. Use right away, or refrigerate or freeze the stock for future use.

3. The stock can be stored, covered, in the refrigerator for up to 5 days. If the stock is unused after 5 days, bring it to a boil and reskim before using.

Veal Stock

Yields 2 quarts

WHAT YOU'LL NEED

7 pounds veal bones, cut into 2-inch pieces
    (your butcher will do this for you)

1 6-ounce can tomato paste

4 medium tomatoes, washed and cut into wedges

3 stalks celery, washed and cut into 1-inch pieces

4 carrots, washed, peeled, and cut into 1-inch pieces

1 bulb fennel, washed and cut into 1-inch pieces

2 cups dry red wine

1 tablespoon whole black peppercorns

5 cloves garlic, peeled and coarsely chopped

3 bay leaves

4 sprigs fresh thyme

1 gallon water

WHAT TO DO

1. Preheat the oven to 400 degrees. Place the bones in a large roasting pan and roast until golden brown, about 45 minutes. Do not burn them.

2. Remove the pan from the oven and brush the bones with the tomato paste. Scatter the vegetables over the bones. Return the pan to the oven and roast for 30 more minutes.

3. Remove the pan from the oven and place it on the stove. Remove the bones and vegetables from the hot pan and put them in a large stockpot. Add the red wine to the hot pan and stir to remove the scrapings from the bottom.

4. Add the wine and scrapings to the stockpot along with the peppercorns, garlic, herbs, and water. Bring the liquid to a boil, then reduce the heat for a low simmer, so that one or two bubbles break the surface of the stock about once a minute. Simmer, uncovered, for 4 to 5 hours.

5. Remove the pot from the heat and skim off any impurities that have risen to the surface. Pour the stock through a strainer into a plastic container or large bowl and discard the solids. Use the stock right away, or refrigerate or freeze it for future use.

6. The stock can be refrigerated, covered, for up to 5 days. If it is not used after 5 days, bring it to a boil and reskim before using.

Vegetable Broth

Yields 3 quarts

WHAT YOU'LL NEED

2 tomatoes, washed and cut into wedges

1 onion, peeled and cut into quarters

1 leek (white part only), washed and cut in half lengthwise

2 shallots, peeled and coarsely chopped

4 cloves garlic, peeled and coarsely chopped

2 stalks celery, washed and cut into 1-inch pieces

1 carrot, washed, peeled, and cut into 1-inch pieces

1 bulb fennel, washed and cut into quarters

1 cup fresh mushrooms, washed and cut into quarters
    (use entire mushroom)

1 small bunch flat-leaf parsley

1 small bunch fresh thyme or 1 teaspoon dried

2 bay leaves

3 whole cloves

About 4 quarts water

Kosher salt and freshly ground white pepper to taste (use black if you don't have white)

WHAT TO DO

1. Add the tomatoes, onion, leek, shallots, garlic, celery, carrot, fennel, mushrooms, parsley, thyme, bay leaves, and cloves to a large stockpot. Add water to cover. Bring to a boil over high heat. Reduce the heat; skim to remove any impurities and foam that rise to the top.

2. Simmer on low heat so that one or two bubbles break the surface of the broth about once a minute, uncovered, for 1½ hours. Season with salt and pepper. Pour the broth through a strainer into a large bowl and store, covered, in the refrigerator up to 1 week, or freeze.

Mushroom Stock

Yields 1 quart

WHAT YOU'LL NEED

4 cups water

1 pound assorted fresh mushrooms, washed and quartered

1 bay leaf

1 large onion, peeled and cut into quarters

4 cloves garlic, peeled and chopped

6 tablespoons unsalted butter

6 tablespoons all-purpose flour

½ cup half-and-half

Kosher salt and freshly ground white pepper to taste

WHAT TO DO

1. Bring the water to a boil in a 2-quart pot. Add the mushrooms, bay leaf, onion, and garlic. Reduce the heat. Simmer on low heat so that one or two bubbles break the surface of the stock about once a minute, covered, for at least 1 hour.

2. Make a roux: Melt the butter in a large heavy-bottomed pot over medium heat. Add the flour and whisk until the mixture is smooth and the roux has darkened to a medium brown. Continue to whisk while slowly adding the half-and-half. Stir constantly until the sauce is thick and smooth.

3. Remove the bay leaf from the mushroom stock and discard. Add the mushroom stock to the roux very slowly and stir until evenly incorporated. Season with salt and pepper to taste.

APPETIZERS

Appetizers are a great way to entertain family and friends before dinner. While cooking in many great restaurants, I learned that almost any dish can be refined into a magical little appetizer. In the summer my wife and I enjoy having people over to sit around the pool and eat chips 'n' dip or my chilled watermelon cubes marinated in passion fruit Cognac. But you can take almost anything big and make it small: Seasonal soups can be served as appetizers in little espresso cups; beef, tuna, or burgers can be made into tiny sliders; the leaves of endive or iceberg lettuce can be filled with something savory; turkey and steak satays are great all-year-round; and then there are chicken wings, the best of all!

Crispy Crab Cakes

Like lobster, crab must be cooked while still alive. Most home cooks don't buy live crabs, and to tell you the truth, the process of cooking and cleaning live crabs can be intimidating. But the good news is that you can buy Maryland lump crabmeat and other sorts of crab frozen or precooked at local grocery stores, or you can order it online. Either way, it will be just fine for these crab cakes. Drain the liquid from the crabmeat but save a little in case the cakes are too dry to shape easily. Pick the crab clean and discard all bits of shell and cartilage. For breading mixture, use crumbled homemade or store-bought cornbread, or you can even use crumbled Ritz Crackers or dried bread crumbs.

Serves 4

WHAT YOU'LL NEED

2 large eggs

3 tablespoons mayonnaise

2 tablespoons sour cream

1 teaspoon Dijon mustard

2 tablespoons barbecue sauce

3 dashes of Tabasco sauce

1 pound lump crabmeat, picked over for shells
and cartilage

Kosher salt and freshly ground pepper to taste

⅓ cup minced red bell pepper

⅓ cup minced red onion

3½ tablespoons finely chopped fresh cilantro leaves

Grated zest and juice of 1 lemon

1½ cups dried cornbread crumbs for filling and
breading

3 tablespoons canola oil

1. Combine the eggs, mayonnaise, sour cream, mustard, barbecue sauce, and Tabasco in a mixing bowl. (Note: If the crab is very moist, you may not need all of this egg mixture.)

2. Preheat the oven to 350 degrees.

3. Using a spoon, gently fold three-quarters of the egg mixture into the crab. Season the crab with salt and pepper as you mix it. Mix in the pepper, onion, cilantro, lemon zest and juice, but be careful not to overmix; you want the crab to be as lumpy as possible. Gently fold in the remaining egg mixture now if you need it.

4. Add enough cornbread crumbs to the mixture to absorb excess moisture. The mixture should be just firm enough to hold together. Taste the mixture and adjust the seasonings. Form into medium-sized crab cakes (about 2½ inches in diameter). Cover and refrigerate the cakes for 15 minutes.

5. Remove the crab cakes from the refrigerator and dust both sides with cornbread crumbs.

6. Heat the canola oil in a sauté pan over medium heat. Working in batches if necessary, add the crab cakes to the oil and fry until crispy brown on both sides. Place the crab cakes on a baking sheet and bake in the 350-degree oven for 12 to 15 minutes. Remove and drain on paper towels and serve immediately.

WHAT'S THE STORY

I love Maryland lump crabmeat partly because it is so versatile. When I was at Café Bellagio, I encrusted sea bass with seasoned crab, and I also used it in my granddaddy's version of New Orleans gumbo when I manned the stoves at Caesars Palace Buffet. In making crab cakes for clients and friends, I use crumbled sweet skillet cornbread to hold the cakes together. Try it. These cakes are so light and delicious that you won't ever be tempted to go back to standard bread crumbs.

Marinated Watermelon Cubes

The best watermelons are the seedless variety you find at their peak in the summer. If you want to make sure that a melon is ripe, thump it with your knuckle. If you hear a hollow drumlike sound, that melon is ready for you.

Serves 4 to 6

WHAT YOU'LL NEED

8 ounces seedless watermelon

½ cup passion fruit vodka or Cognac

1 medium orange, rind and pith removed,
    flesh minced

4 large strawberries, washed, hulled, and finely chopped

8 fresh mint leaves, thinly sliced

WHAT TO DO

1. Cut the red fruit of the watermelon from the rind and cut into 1-inch cubes. Set aside in a 2-inch-deep pie plate.

2. Drizzle each cube with vodka or Cognac and set in the refrigerator to chill. Let the watermelon marinate for at least 1 hour, and as long as overnight.

3. Place the orange, strawberries, and mint in a sieve to remove the excess juice. Toss gently and set aside.

4. Remove the watermelon cubes from the refrigerator and put them on a serving plate. Using a small spoon, place a small amount of the minted fruit topping on each cube and serve.

WHAT'S THE STORY

Like a lot of kids, I believed that if I swallowed a watermelon seed, a watermelon would grow in my stomach, but that never stopped my sister and me from loving the best fruit on earth. As a chef in some of the finest restaurants on the West Coast, I made it my mission to give the watermelon a makeover and take it upscale. I cubed it, marinated it in passion fruit vodka or Cognac, and topped it off with minted citrus. These little cubes are great for parties, especially backyard barbecues.

"Dip 'n' Chips" Chunky Spicy Avocado

This dip can be served on tacos, burgers, steaks, or even with nacho cheese Doritos.

Serves 4 to 6

WHAT YOU'LL NEED

5 large ripe Hass avocados

1 cup finely diced red onion

½ cup fresh cilantro leaves, washed and finely chopped, plus sprigs for garnish

1 teaspoon minced jalapeño pepper

Juice of 1 lime

6 tablespoons extra-virgin olive oil

Kosher salt and freshly ground pepper to taste

2 large tomatoes, washed, seeded, and finely diced

4 cups canola oil

15 6-inch corn tortillas, cut into quarters

1 lime, thinly sliced

WHAT TO DO

1. Peel and pit the avocados. Place them in a glass bowl and mash with a fork, leaving some chunks.

2. Add the onion, chopped cilantro, jalapeño, lime juice, olive oil, and salt and pepper to taste. Continue mashing until all is incorporated but the mixture is still lumpy. Gently fold in the tomatoes.

3. Heat the canola oil in a large saucepan to 375 degrees or until a piece of tortilla sizzles when you drop it in. Fry the tortillas a few at a time until crisp, about 2 minutes.

4. Drain on paper towels and season with salt. The chips can be prepared up to 2 days ahead and stored covered.

5. To serve, spoon the avocado mixture into a serving bowl and garnish with cilantro sprigs. Place the bowl on a large serving plate and scatter the corn chips around it. Add lime slices as garnish. Serve immediately.

WHAT'S THE STORY

Growing up, we always had avocados in our house. My granddaddy even had an avocado tree in his yard that doubled as a swing for the grandchildren. Granddaddy served avocados sliced and seasoned with salt and pepper or sometimes drizzled with Italian dressing. He also picked them, let them ripen in brown paper bags, and gave them to family members.

Grilled Chicken Wings

This is a healthier version of my original chicken wing recipe. Spice them up, put them in the oven or on the grill, and serve with mixed greens drizzled with light herb vinaigrette, or with steamed white rice and a side of seasoned sliced avocado.

Serves 4 to 6

WHAT YOU'LL NEED

3 tablespoons olive oil

2 teaspoons grated lemon zest

1½ tablespoons fresh lemon juice

3 cloves garlic, peeled and finely minced

1½ teaspoons kosher salt, plus additional to taste

1 tablespoon freshly ground pepper, plus additional to taste

2 teaspoons cayenne pepper

3 pounds chicken wings, washed and
    wing tips tucked at the joint

WHAT TO DO

1. Combine the oil, lemon zest, lemon juice, garlic, salt, pepper, and cayenne in a large bowl; stir well. Add the chicken and toss to coat. Cover and marinate in the refrigerator for at least 4 hours or overnight.

2. If using a charcoal grill, prepare the grill first by oiling the grill rack with canola oil and a towel and then prepare a solid bed of medium-hot coals. For a gas grill, preheat to high with the lid closed, then open the lid and reduce the heat to medium. You should be able to hold your hand 1 to 2 inches above the grill rack for just 4 to 5 seconds.

3. Lay the chicken wings on the grill rack. If using a charcoal grill, place them on the medium-hot area of the grill; if using a gas grill, close the lid to cook. Cook for 8 to 12 minutes on each side, turning the wings once, until the skin is browned and crisp and the meat is tender and juicy (cut into a wing to taste for doneness and flavor). If necessary, cook 2 to 3 minutes longer on each side.

WHAT'S THE STORY

To me wings are the best part of the chicken—those bones mean flavor and juicy meat! You can fry them, barbecue them, bake them, make soup with them, or stuff them. When Friendly and I had our little chicken business back in the day, our customers never got wings because Friendly would eat them all while we were frying up the rest of the chicken parts. You can eat wings hot, warm, or even cold along with chips and dip or mashed potatoes. Make 'em spicy!

Barbecued Chicken Wings

Here's a favorite recipe I make in the spring and summer months. I prep these wings the way I prep the baked and grilled versions. Get your bib out and have a wet towel ready; my Smoked Molasses Barbecue Sauce really sets these wings off. Oh, and by the way, while the wings are on the grill, foil-wrap some fresh corn on the cob and some yams and put them on the grill, too. That's the ultimate backyard dinner.

Serves 8

WHAT YOU'LL NEED

3 tablespoons extra-virgin olive oil

1½ tablespoons fresh lemon juice

3 cloves garlic, peeled and finely minced

2 tablespoons finely chopped fresh cilantro leaves

1½ tablespoons kosher salt

1 tablespoon freshly ground pepper

3 pounds chicken wings, washed and
    wing tips tucked at the joint

3 cups Smoked Molasses Barbecue Sauce
    (page 42)

WHAT TO DO

1. Combine the olive oil, lemon juice, garlic, cilantro, salt, and pepper in a large bowl; stir well. Add the chicken and toss to coat. Cover and marinate in the refrigerator for at least 4 hours or overnight.

2. Preheat the oven to 375 degrees. Place the wings on a broiler pan lined with aluminum foil. Bake until fork tender and golden brown, 25 to 30 minutes.

3. Toss the wings with the barbecue sauce in a large bowl and serve immediately.

East Coast Buffalo Wings

Buffalo wings got their name from a bar in Buffalo, New York, or so the story goes. Several people claim credit for their creation. I like to make them a little less spicy than most other versions. I also like them sweet—that's why I've added honey here. Anything goes with these party favorites—fries, chips, cole slaw, or potato salad. We like to serve them with all of those things.

Serves 6 to 8

WHAT YOU'LL NEED

> 3 pounds chicken wings, washed and
> > wing tips tucked at the joint
>
> 3 cups canola oil
>
> 4 tablespoons (½ stick) unsalted butter
>
> ⅓ cup hot pepper sauce
>
> 2 tablespoons fresh lemon juice
>
> 2 tablespoons honey
>
> 1½ tablespoons kosher salt
>
> 1 tablespoon freshly ground pepper
>
> Carrot and celery sticks
>
> ½ cup Creamy Blue Cheese Dressing (page 91)

WHAT TO DO

1. Pat dry the chicken wings.

2. Heat the oil in a large pot to a medium-high temperature. Test a wing in the oil; if it begins to sizzle, the oil is ready. Deep-fry the wings in batches for 12 to 15 minutes. Drain well on paper towels. Or bake them in a preheated 350-degree oven until fork tender and golden brown, about 25 minutes.

3. Melt the butter in a saucepan, then stir in the hot sauce, lemon juice, and honey. Simmer the sauce for 8 to 10 minutes. Remove and set aside.

4. Gently toss the wings with the hot sauce in a large bowl. Season with the salt and pepper. Serve the wings with carrot and celery sticks and Creamy Blue Cheese Dressing.

Garlic-Ginger-Tequila Chicken Drumettes

If you cut a chicken wing into segments at the joint, you get one segment that is really meaty, called a *drumette*. Drumettes are easy to fix, and you can often find them already cut at the grocery store. Here it's the ginger that gives these Mexican wings their kick. The tequila and fresh cilantro balance the spicy kick with a cool flavor. Have wedges of fresh lime ready to squeeze over the wings. And you know what's great with these drumettes? Warm corn tortillas.

Serves 6

WHAT YOU'LL NEED

⅓ cup low-sodium soy sauce

⅓ cup tequila

2 tablespoons finely minced fresh ginger

2 cloves garlic, peeled and finely minced

1 tablespoon finely chopped fresh cilantro leaves

1 tablespoon toasted sesame oil

1 teaspoon brown sugar

1 teaspoon rice vinegar

⅛ teaspoon cayenne pepper

3 pounds chicken drumettes, washed

WHAT TO DO

1. Combine all the ingredients except the chicken in a large bowl. Stir well with a whisk or fork.

2. Add the drumettes to the mixture and toss well to coat. Cover and refrigerate for 2 hours or more, tossing occasionally.

3. Remove the drumettes from the marinade. Line a large baking pan with aluminum foil.

4. Preheat the oven to 375 degrees. Arrange the wings in the baking pan in a single layer. Cook in batches if necessary. Bake, turning the wings once, until golden brown and fork tender, 10 to 12 minutes on each side.

Barbecued Shrimp Scampi

This is a simple recipe for lunch or dinner. If you don't have shrimp, use scallops or lobster tails, or just make the sauce and serve it with a nice piece of white fish. One quick note: Don't leave the sauce unattended on the stove. Set the heat under it at low to medium so the sauce doesn't separate. If you want traditional scampi, just don't add the barbecue sauce. Potato salad and grilled corn on the cob go well with this dish.

Serves 4

WHAT YOU'LL NEED

6 to 8 tablespoons unsalted butter

12 jumbo shrimp, peeled, deveined, and washed

$\frac{1}{3}$ cup finely chopped yellow onion

2 tablespoons finely minced garlic

$\frac{1}{4}$ cup white wine

Grated zest and juice of 1 lemon

$\frac{1}{3}$ cup diced and seeded tomatoes

2 tablespoons finely chopped flat-leaf parsley

Kosher salt and freshly ground white pepper to taste

$\frac{1}{4}$ cup Smoked Molasses Barbecue Sauce (page 42)

WHAT TO DO

1. Melt 2 tablespoons of the butter in a medium sauté pan over medium heat. Add the shrimp, onion, and garlic and sauté for 3 to 4 minutes. The shrimp will begin to plump up a bit.

2. Add the wine, lemon zest and juice, and 4 tablespoons more butter. Reduce the heat and gently sauté the shrimp until the sauce thickens. If the sauce is too thin, add 1 to 2 tablespoons more butter.

3. Add the tomatoes and parsley and season with salt and pepper to taste.

4. Add the barbecue sauce and toss well. To serve, remove the shrimp from the pan with a fork, place on plates, and drizzle the sauce over the shrimp with a spoon.

WHAT'S THE STORY

Every restaurant I've worked in has had some kind of scampi dish on the menu. I wanted to re-create this classic European favorite by finishing it off with my smoked molasses barbecue sauce. Does that take this classic to another level? See for yourself. Just don't forget to add my barbecue sauce to get that special flavor.

Crispy Shrimp, Oysters, and Chips

Here's another favorite summer dish, especially when I'm down home in the Big Easy with my family. I once made a fancy version at the Bellagio during an in-house "iron chef" competition against the hotel's other restaurants. I served it on top-of-the-line china with sterling silver forks. The crispy shrimp and oysters were sprinkled with fresh chives and accompanied by homemade potato chips and Granny Smith apple tartar sauce. The judges loved the dish, and Café Bellagio won the competition. This is the home version. Add some catfish tenders or any other seafood you like. You can buy oysters that have been shucked of their shells at many markets.

Serves 4

WHAT YOU'LL NEED

4 cups canola oil

16 large oysters, shucked

16 medium shrimp, peeled, deveined, and
    washed

Kosher salt and freshly ground pepper

4 large eggs

⅓ cup whole milk

½ cup cornmeal

1 cup all-purpose flour

1 teaspoon cayenne pepper

1½ tablespoons finely chopped
    fresh chives

5 large russet potatoes, peeled, washed, and
    thinly sliced

Spicy Tartar Sauce (page 45)

WHAT TO DO

1. In a deep-fryer or a large pot, heat the oil to 350 degrees. Test the oil temperature with an oyster or shrimp. If the shellfish begins to fry without the oil bubbling and popping, the oil is ready.

2. On a plate lined with paper towels, season the oysters and shrimp with salt and pepper. Set aside.

3. Add the eggs and milk to a large bowl and whisk thoroughly together. Season with a pinch each of salt and pepper. Add the seasoned oysters and shrimp and coat well.

4. Mix the cornmeal, flour, and cayenne in a second large bowl. Stir 1 tablespoon each salt and pepper into the flour mixture.

5. Add the oysters and shrimp to the cornmeal mixture and coat well. Set the seafood aside on a plate lined with paper towels.

6. Using a pair of tongs, drop the breaded oysters and shrimp into the oil in small batches. Deep-fry until cooked through and golden brown, 8 to 10 minutes. Remove and drain on paper towels. Garnish with the chives.

7. For the potato chips, very thinly slice the potatoes using a handheld slicer. If you don't plan to fry the potatoes right away, keep them in a bowl filled with water. Pat dry before frying.

8. Deep-fry the potato chips in batches until crispy golden brown, 10 to 12 minutes. Remove from the oil with a slotted spoon and drain on paper towels. Season with salt. Serve the seafood and chips with Spicy Tartar Sauce.

Grilled Marinated Turkey and Steak Satays

It's party time with these marinated turkey and steak satays. You can serve these appetizers with any kind of dipping sauce, but I recommend my peanut sauce for the turkey and my cilantro pesto for the steak. Back-in-the-Day Creamed Corn Sauce (page 39) holds its own with both satays. These satays can be made with any type of poultry or beef.

Serves 4 to 6

WHAT YOU'LL NEED

24 to 28 small or medium bamboo skewers

1½ cups Spicy Cilantro Pesto (page 41)

1 pound turkey tenders or 3-ounce strips, cut
    into 4 by 1 inch strips

1 pound skirt steak, cleaned and cut into
    4- by 1-inch strips

½ cup Chunky Peanut Sauce (page 43)

3 tablespoons finely chopped fresh cilantro leaves

WHAT TO DO

1. Soak the skewers in water to cover. This will keep them from burning when you grill the satays.

2. Divide 1 cup of the cilantro pesto between 2 medium bowls, saving the remaining ½ cup for dipping later. Add the turkey to one bowl and steak to the other. Coat both meats well. Cover tightly and refrigerate for several hours or overnight.

3. On a plastic or glass dish, thread the marinated meats onto the skewers and cover.

4. Prepare a charcoal grill or preheat a gas grill. Have tongs ready for turning the satays.

5. Grill the skewered meats, turning for consistent cooking and grill marks, for 4 to 6 minutes total cooking time.

6. Place the skewers on a serving plate with the wooden ends facing the rim of the plate. Pour the peanut sauce into a small ramekin and the remaining cilantro pesto into another ramekin, place in the center of the plate, and garnish with fresh cilantro. Serve immediately.

Spicy Turkey Chili

Here's a dish I love, especially in the winter. People usually think of chili as a beef-based dish, but you can use turkey or chicken too. At Café Bellagio, we diced beef tenderloin tips to make an upscale version.

Serves 6 to 8

WHAT YOU'LL NEED

3 tablespoons vegetable oil

1½ pounds lean ground turkey

1½ cups coarsely chopped yellow onion

½ cup coarsely chopped green bell pepper

1½ tablespoons minced garlic

2 tablespoons chili powder

2 teaspoons ground cumin

1 teaspoon salt

¼ teaspoon freshly ground pepper

2 medium tomatoes, washed and
    coarsely chopped

3 tablespoons tomato paste

1 teaspoon sugar

2 cups water

1 cup grated smoked Cheddar cheese

1 bunch scallions (tops only), washed and
    coarsely chopped

WHAT TO DO

1. Heat 1 tablespoon of the oil in a medium pot with a heavy bottom over medium-high heat. Add the meat and stir with a large wooden spoon to break it up. Cook, stirring, until the meat is browned and cooked through, 8 to 10 minutes.

2. Transfer the meat to a strainer to drain off liquid.

3. Set the pot over medium-high heat. Add the remaining 2 tablespoons oil, the onion, bell pepper, and garlic. Cook for 6 to 8 minutes. Return the ground turkey to the pot and mix well.

4. Add the chili powder, cumin, salt, and pepper and cook, stirring, for about 2 minutes. Add the tomatoes, tomato paste, sugar, and water. Stir well and bring to a boil. Reduce the heat to medium-low and simmer, uncovered, for about 30 minutes. Taste for flavor and add salt and pepper if needed. Keep warm on the stove until ready to serve.

5. To serve, spoon the chili into individual bowls, top with smoked Cheddar cheese, and garnish with scallions. And my Cakelike Cornbread (page 199) goes great with this chili dish.

Granddaddy in the Kitchen

There was a sign over the kitchen door that said "Charlie's Kitchen" and it wasn't a joke. Granddaddy cooked mostly on the weekends—Friday dinner, Saturday dinner, and a big meal after church on Sunday—and while he was cooking, hardly anyone was welcome. The best you could do to pass through the kitchen was to boost his ego a little first: "Granddaddy, that sure smells good!" But standing around watching and trying to taste? I don't think so.

So my first experience of all the rules that cooks and chefs like to lay down in their kitchens came from him. For one thing, Granddaddy wouldn't ever let you serve yourself. He didn't want anyone picking out the things they liked best from his gumbo or choosing their favorite chicken pieces. He served. You ate. And if you moved anything in his refrigerator during the week, he was bound to give you a talking-to.

Granddaddy worked with one wooden-handled knife that he sharpened himself. With that one knife he could do almost anything, including fillet the fish he bought from the Los Angeles market that advertised "You buy. We fry." He bought, but he fried his own—cleaned it too.

All the discipline that Granddaddy showed in running his weekday janitorial business carried over to his work in the kitchen on weekends. He was a clean dresser, really detail oriented about his clothes, and he always wore an apron while he cooked. I may not have thought much about this at the time, but I know it had an impact on me because I remember his ways and I appreciate them now.

What did we eat? Fridays might be a fish fry with potato salad and lettuce and tomato. Saturdays maybe he'd make bell peppers stuffed with beef and rice or smothered steak or baked chicken. On Sundays he might make a gumbo or meat loaf. And there was always avocado from his tree in the yard.

We were living in Los Angeles, but our roots were back in New Orleans where he and my grandmother grew up and started their family. His food never lost track of that. I guess that not forgetting where I come from is something else I get from him.

Many years later, I came home from my first job working for Robert Gadsby and was eager to show off everything I was learning. I'd made it through a life-changing period, I'd got a job with one of the top Los Angeles chefs, and I wanted my family to be proud. So

Granddaddy let me use the kitchen to show off my cooking, and while I did, he interrupted every three or four minutes with his instructions. I don't remember too much about the rest of the meal, but I can still laugh about the dessert. I made banana tempura, which I put on skewers interspersed with strawberries. I crisscrossed the skewers on the plates, and because there wasn't any mint, I garnished them with bits of green scallion!

I don't know if my family was impressed by my presentation or my food, but Granddaddy ate it and that was a compliment because he refused to eat anything except what he or my grandmother cooked at home. I wish I could have persuaded him to come out to my restaurants to see his grandson in action, but I know he was proud of me.

SAUCES AND CONDIMENTS

No dish is complete without some type of condiment or sauce to enhance its flavor. That drizzle of sauce or dash of condiment is the finishing touch that brings out the best in your creations. Both condiments and sauces can be created from a wide range of ingredients you probably already have in your icebox or pantry. Tomatoes can be turned into salsa, into tomato jam for chips and dip, or into a spread for a sandwich. Avocados can be made into chunky guacamole. Simple sauces can be made from vegetables like corn, broccoli, or asparagus by blanching the vegetables and pureeing them with additional vegetables, low-sodium chicken broth, butter, cream, and salt and pepper. I am sharing a few of my favorite sauces and condiments here. Master them first and then play around with creating your own.

Back-in-the-Day Creamed Corn

You don't see creamed corn around much these days, but it's something I really enjoyed when I was growing up. We always had the canned version, and my sister would add a touch of sugar to sweeten it a bit. Creamed corn goes well with any meat; I especially like it with fried chicken or crab cakes. Messing around in the kitchen with my former cook Timmy during my days at Caesars Palace, I learned to make it from scratch. You can also use this recipe to make a great sauce for fish.

Serves 4

WHAT YOU'LL NEED

7 ears corn, shucked

8 tablespoons (1 stick) unsalted butter

½ cup coarsely chopped yellow onion

3 cloves garlic, peeled and finely minced

Kosher salt and freshly ground white pepper to taste

1½ cups low-sodium chicken broth

¼ cup heavy (whipping) cream

WHAT TO DO

1. Remove the corn kernels by holding the cob upright and slicing the kernels from the cob with a sharp knife.

2. Melt 3 tablespoons of the butter in a medium saucepan over medium-high heat. Add the corn, onion, garlic, and a pinch each of salt and pepper. Sauté until the vegetables are soft, 6 to 8 minutes.

3. Add the chicken broth and let the corn cook for 10 to 12 minutes, keeping the corn sauce at a gentle simmer. Taste for salt and pepper after 10 minutes. Remove from the heat.

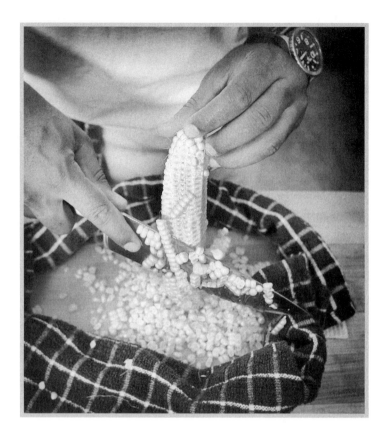

4. Pour half the corn mixture into a blender (do not fill the blender more than halfway). Puree until smooth, slowly adding cream until the sauce is the desired consistency. Repeat with the remaining corn and cream. For a smoother texture, pour through a strainer to remove the kernels. Serve immediately, or let cool and refrigerate in an airtight container until chilled.

Spicy Cilantro Pesto

This is a version of pesto made with cilantro instead of basil. The cilantro gives it a kick that, to my mind, makes it more versatile than traditional pesto. You can use it as a marinade for meats, dip satays in it, or serve it drizzled on some tacos.

Serves 4 to 6

WHAT YOU'LL NEED

2 cups cilantro leaves, washed and finely chopped

½ cup spinach, cooked and chopped

1 small jalapeño pepper, seeded and finely chopped

1 clove garlic, peeled and finely chopped

1 cup plus 2 tablespoons extra-virgin olive oil

Juice from 1 lemon

Kosher salt to taste

WHAT TO DO

1. In a blender, puree the cilantro, spinach, jalapeño, garlic, olive oil, and lemon juice until smooth.

2. Season to taste with salt. Place in an airtight jar and keep refrigerated until ready to serve.

WHAT'S THE STORY

I learned how to make this sauce back in my early days as a line cook. We served it with cured Meyer lemon on striped bass. The fragrant lemon and cilantro went beautifully with the fish, petite potatoes, Vichy carrots, and black beluga lentils. This is a perfect example of taking simple ingredients and turning them into sensational components of a dish.

Smoked Molasses Barbecue Sauce

This is a great barbecue sauce for the home cook. It's easy to make and has a good shelf life. Naturally it's perfect for ribs and chicken, but don't rule it out as a dipping sauce for my satays. Even my Crispy Crab Cakes (page 13) are great with this sauce.

Serves 4 to 6

WHAT YOU'LL NEED

4 tablespoons (½ stick) unsalted butter

½ cup finely chopped yellow onion

1 clove garlic, peeled and finely chopped

1⅓ cups ketchup

½ cup apple cider vinegar

1 tablespoon Worcestershire sauce

1 teaspoon liquid smoke

1 cup (packed) dark brown sugar

1 tablespoon Tabasco sauce

¼ cup molasses

Kosher salt and freshly ground pepper to taste

WHAT TO DO

1. Melt the butter in a medium saucepan over medium heat. Add the onion and garlic and cook until softened, 6 to 8 minutes.

2. Add the ketchup, vinegar, Worcestershire sauce, liquid smoke, and brown sugar. Stir until fully incorporated and bring to a simmer. Add the Tabasco and molasses. Simmer 25 to 30 minutes. Season with salt and pepper to taste. The barbecue sauce should be medium thick.

3. Let the sauce cool for about 1 hour, then pour into a blender and puree until smooth. Serve warm or at room temperature. Store in an airtight container in the refrigerator.

Chunky Peanut Sauce

Anytime I make turkey satays, I want to have my to-die-for chunky peanut sauce. It also goes well with chicken or fish. You can use smooth peanut butter if you prefer; just don't be afraid of this great but unusual combination.

Serves 4 to 6

WHAT YOU'LL NEED

½ cup coconut milk

2 tablespoons red curry paste

½ cup chunky peanut butter

½ cup low-fat milk

3 tablespoons brown sugar

2 tablespoons fresh lime juice

½ teaspoon kosher salt

WHAT TO DO

1. Pour the coconut milk into a small saucepan. Stirring occasionally, heat the milk over medium heat until it reaches a gentle simmer and tiny beads of oil glisten on the surface, about 5 minutes.

2. Add the curry paste and whisk until it dissolves, about 3 minutes. Add the peanut butter, milk, and brown sugar and gently cook, stirring, until the sauce is smooth, about 5 minutes.

3. Remove from the heat and season with lime juice and salt to taste. Cool to room temperature and serve. The sauce, covered in an airtight container, can be refrigerated for up to 3 days.

Spicy Chicken Salsa

Salsas are much more versatile than most people realize. This one is great with chips, of course, but try making it without the chicken and serving it as a condiment with fish. You'll see what I mean.

Serves 4 to 6

WHAT YOU'LL NEED

6 ounces grilled seasoned chicken breast, finely chopped

4 ripe tomatoes, washed, seeded, and finely diced

2 cloves garlic, peeled and finely chopped

1 jalapeño pepper, seeded and finely chopped

1 tablespoon finely chopped fresh cilantro leaves

Juice of ½ lime

1½ tablespoons extra-virgin olive oil

Kosher salt to taste

WHAT TO DO

Place the chicken, tomatoes, garlic, jalapeño, and cilantro in a medium bowl. Gently fold the ingredients together. Stir in the lime juice and oil and season with salt to taste.

Spicy Tartar Sauce

This quick and easy dipping sauce for fish and chips would also be a great spread for an oyster po' boy. At Café Bellagio we made a tartar sauce with Granny Smith apples, which gave the sauce great texture and a nice tartness.

Serves 4 to 6

WHAT YOU'LL NEED

1 cup mayonnaise

1 tablespoon Dijon mustard

1 tablespoon minced green olives

1 tablespoon minced capers

1 tablespoon finely chopped red onions

1 tablespoon finely chopped dill pickle

3 tablespoons finely chopped fresh chives

2 tablespoons finely chopped flat-leaf parsley

1 tablespoon fresh lemon juice

Tabasco sauce to taste

WHAT TO DO

1. Place all the ingredients except the Tabasco in a medium bowl and gently fold together.

2. Season with Tabasco. Refrigerate, tightly covered, until ready to serve.

Cole Slaw

I like to mix Savoy and red cabbages in this cole slaw for their different colors, flavors, and textures. Serve it as a side dish at a barbecue or put it on a burger or a sandwich. You make the call.

Serves 4 to 6

WHAT YOU'LL NEED

1 head Savoy cabbage, washed, cored, and finely shredded

½ head red cabbage, washed, cored, and finely shredded

2 large carrots, washed, peeled, and finely shredded

¾ cup mayonnaise

2 tablespoons sour cream

2 tablespoons grated Spanish onion

2 tablespoons sugar, or to taste

2 tablespoons distilled white vinegar

1 tablespoon dry mustard

2 teaspoons celery salt

Kosher salt and freshly ground pepper to taste

WHAT TO DO

1. Combine the shredded cabbages and carrots in a large bowl. In a separate bowl, whisk together the mayonnaise, sour cream, onion, sugar, vinegar, mustard, celery salt, salt, and pepper, then add to the cabbage mixture.

2. Mix well to combine. Taste for seasoning; add more salt, pepper, or sugar if desired.

My grandfather, Charles Henderson Sr., and my grandmother, Ethel Mae Henderson, barbecuing on Labor Day in the backyard of our family home.

Smoky Ketchup

This kicked-up version of ketchup is great on burgers, fries, and even fish and chips. Just add liquid smoke and honey to a bottle of ketchup and you have a slammin' condiment.

Yields approximately 1 cup

WHAT YOU'LL NEED

> 1 cup ketchup
> ¼ teaspoon liquid smoke
> 1 tablespoon honey
> Pinch cayenne pepper
> Freshly ground pepper to taste

WHAT TO DO

Whisk the ketchup, liquid smoke, honey, and cayenne pepper together in a small bowl. Season to taste with pepper.

Garlic-Herb Marinade

Use this vinaigrette as either a salad dressing or a marinade for meat or vegetables. You can also drizzle a bit of it on cooked meat, fish, or vegetables.

Yields 2 cups

WHAT YOU'LL NEED

6 large cloves garlic, peeled and finely minced

2 tablespoons finely chopped fresh thyme

3 tablespoons finely chopped fresh rosemary

½ teaspoon dried red chili flakes

½ cup fresh lemon juice

1½ cups extra-virgin olive oil

Kosher salt and freshly ground pepper to taste

WHAT TO DO

Whisk the garlic, thyme, rosemary, chili flakes, lemon juice, and oil together in a medium bowl. Season with salt and pepper. The marinade can be made 1 day ahead and stored in the refrigerator.

Candied Walnuts

These walnuts are like candy and add a nice texture to my Field Greens and Apple Salad (page 79). They can also be served with ice cream and many of the desserts at the end of this book. At Café Bellagio I had to hide the candied walnuts from the staff or they'd disappear. So don't leave them around if you want them to last. After you make these a few times, try making candied pecans.

Serves 4 to 6

WHAT YOU'LL NEED

2 large egg whites

2 teaspoons water

¾ cup walnut halves

1 cup superfine sugar

2 teaspoons salt

1 teaspoon cayenne pepper

WHAT TO DO

1. Preheat the oven to 250 degrees. Beat the egg whites and water together in a mixing bowl. Add the nuts and stir until completely coated. Drain well in a strainer or colander.

2. Combine the sugar, salt, and cayenne and toss the nuts in this mixture until evenly coated. Turn onto a baking sheet lined with wax paper and spread in a single layer.

3. Bake for 10 minutes, then reduce the oven temperature to 225 degrees. Bake, stirring occasionally, until the nuts are dark brown, about 10 minutes more. Let cool completely before serving.

4. Store in an airtight container for up to 2 weeks.

Chunky Guacamole

Here's a condiment for any occasion—from a party to an evening at home watching a movie. Just be sure the avocados are nice and ripe.

Serves 4 to 6

WHAT YOU'LL NEED

6 avocados, peeled and pitted

Juice of 1 lime

3 tablespoons finely diced red onion

2 tablespoons minced seeded jalapeño peppers

3 tablespoons finely chopped fresh cilantro leaves

2 plum tomatoes, washed, seeded, and finely diced

2 tablespoons finely minced garlic

Kosher salt and freshly ground pepper to taste

WHAT TO DO

1. Mash the avocados with a fork in a medium bowl. Add the lime juice, onion, jalapeños, cilantro, tomatoes, garlic, salt, and pepper. Mix well.

2. Serve immediately or refrigerate for 1 hour to let the flavors blend.

Beefsteak Tomato Salsa

This salsa accompanies any fish, chicken, or beef dish. Simple to make, it will keep in the refrigerator for 2 days. Any type of tomato will work if you don't have beefsteak tomatoes.

Serves 4 to 6

WHAT YOU'LL NEED

1½ cups finely diced ripe beefsteak tomatoes

½ cup finely chopped red onion

2 tablespoons peeled and minced garlic

2 tablespoons finely chopped fresh cilantro leaves

1 tablespoon extra-virgin olive oil

2 teaspoons fresh lime juice

1 teaspoon finely minced jalapeño pepper

Kosher salt to taste

WHAT TO DO

Mix all the ingredients together in a medium bowl. Let the salsa set for about 30 minutes. Pour off the excess tomato juice before serving.

Eggplant Caviar

Serves 6 to 8

WHAT YOU'LL NEED

¼ cup extra-virgin olive oil

2 cups diced eggplant, skin on

⅓ cup diced red onion

⅓ cup diced red bell pepper

2 tablespoons minced garlic

2 tablespoons finely chopped flat-leaf parsley

Kosher salt and freshly ground pepper to taste

WHAT TO DO

1. Heat the oil in a medium sauté pan over medium heat. Add the eggplant, onion, bell pepper, and garlic and stir until all the vegetables are coated with oil. Add a few dashes more of oil if needed.

2. Cook, stirring, until the vegetables are tender, 8 to 10 minutes. Toss in the parsley. Season with salt and pepper to taste.

3. Remove from the heat and serve warm over lamb steaks or with grilled fish.

My First Cooking Job

For those of you who never had the pleasure of eating there, Gadsby's was on the corner of Wilshire and La Brea, and Robert Gadsby was not only an outstanding Los Angeles chef but also a man who can still out cook most high-end chefs you can name. He's that good.

It's hard to explain what Robert Gadsby means to me because it goes way, way beyond food. Robert took me in when I was pretty close to jobless. He took a chance on me. Let's start there. He signed me on as a cook at $5.50 an hour, but what I learned from him was worth millions, and, as I said, it was about much more than food and technique.

Robert is a black man and because of that, when he talked to me, I listened without fear. He grew up in England, so he had a different perspective on how a black man should present himself in the food world. Robert made me understand that I had to drop the prison look if people were going to accept me. He let me know I had to run against the stereotype by working hard, being on time, and following through. I also learned how important it is to be organized. Robert is organized and he's a genius with numbers and operations. If you can't run the food and labor costs, you aren't going to run a restaurant. I didn't master numbers at Gadsby's, but I stored away how important they are for a later time when I would better understand them.

I began to follow Robert's polished way of dressing. I bought top-quality chef coats like his, black pants with a permanent crease, and even got a pair of clogs, though I still worried that clogs were strictly for women. I was only a cook, but I looked like a seasoned professional and it helped me get through a lot of doors.

Except for encountering some high-level white-collar felons on the inside, I'd never really been around the sort of very wealthy people who came to Gadsby's. I was tremendously impressed by the way Robert communicated with these folks. He was everyone's equal and he talked to these people on their level . . . or maybe above it in some cases. In that way, and in others, Robert helped me to feel proud and to find a purpose.

After a while Robert began taking me out to eat with him when we finished work. "You can't grow as a chef if you don't go out to eat," he told me. So we ran these little spy missions on other restaurants, something, I learned, that good chefs do. But before we ate, we'd stop off at a bookstore where Robert picked up audio books and tried to get me interested in the speeches of Churchill and other things that seemed a little odd to me. What I did learn was the value of learning and of being well spoken. Eventually he introduced me to the Cook's Library, a shop where I could get my hands on everything written about the world of food.

Robert was a taskmaster and he could be tough, but his plan was solid. "Jeff, I'm going to train you to take other people's jobs," he told me. It's true, there's always someone lurking around aiming for your job, especially in the corporate food world. Robert wanted me to be ready and to be able to take care of myself. I've learned his lessons well.

SOULFUL SOUPS AND CHOWDERS

Soups can be made from many different ingredients in your kitchen, including leftover vegetables, meats, and seafood. And, believe it or not, some soups can also be turned into great sauces. In the many kitchens I have worked in over the years, I've found that the most versatile soup, the one that can be stretched farthest and transformed with the greatest ease, begins with potatoes and onions. Once you go through the very simple steps of making this soup, you can add leftover chicken or beef to make it a hearty dinner. Begin by simply sautéing onions, garlic, and diced potatoes in a little oil. Add a couple of bay leaves and cover with water. Boil until the potatoes are tender, discard the bay leaf, and puree the soup in your blender with a little butter, milk, salt, and black pepper. You can add and subtract from this basic recipe to give it your personal touch.

My granddaddy used to stockpile ingredients for his signature gumbo throughout the year. He'd find some of the ingredients he wanted on sale and freeze them, and our relatives would ship others to him packed in dry ice. Coming up with your own creation is what gives a soup its soul.

The first gourmet soup I learned to make was the lobster bisque at Chef Gary Clauson's restaurant in the Hotel Bel-Air in Los Angeles. It was the specialty of Mario, the most sought-after line cook on the West Coast. People paid a lot of money to eat at the chef's table in the Bel-Air kitchen, where the rich aromatics and Cognac in Mario's bisque filled the air. I prepped the vegetables for Mario while I studied his moves and technique. Eventually I was allowed to make the soup on my own, which really built my confidence. When Mario went on vacation, which was rare, I ran his coveted station and made the sauces and the lobster bisque. That's my soup story. You will discover yours, so get in the kitchen and make some soup!

Sweet Potato Soup

The addition of turkey smoked collard greens makes this soulful soup into a complete meal, and the nutmeg and maple syrup really bring it to life. Served in the right bowl, it can make an impressive presentation. If possible, use freshly grated nutmeg and pure maple syrup. Without a doubt, you will taste the difference. Serve with Turkey Smoked Collard Greens (page 123).

Serves 4 to 6

WHAT YOU'LL NEED

$1\frac{1}{2}$ tablespoons canola oil

1 cup thinly sliced yellow onion

4 sprigs fresh thyme

1 bay leaf

4 cups low-sodium chicken broth

4 cups cubed peeled sweet potatoes or
garnet yams

8 tablespoons (1 stick) unsalted butter

$1\frac{1}{2}$ teaspoons freshly grated nutmeg

1 teaspoon ground cinnamon

2 tablespoons light brown sugar

$\frac{1}{4}$ cup heavy (whipping) cream

Kosher salt and freshly ground pepper to taste

2 tablespoons pure maple syrup

WHAT TO DO

1. Heat the oil in a medium pot over medium-high heat. Add the onion, thyme, and bay leaf and cook until the onion is softened, 5 to 8 minutes. Add the chicken broth and sweet potatoes. Bring to a boil, then reduce the heat and slowly boil until the potatoes are fork tender, 20 to 25 minutes.

2. Pour off the cooking liquid, reserving 2 cups liquid and the potatoes. Discard the bay leaf and thyme.

3. Place the potatoes, butter, nutmeg, cinnamon, and brown sugar in a blender or food processor. Slowly add the reserved cooking liquid while processing until the desired thickness is achieved and all ingredients are incorporated.

4. Slowly add the cream, then season to taste with salt and pepper and add the maple syrup. Serve immediately.

King Crab Gumbo

Alaskan king crab is huge, spiny, and full of meat. In most stores you will find king crab legs frozen. Thawed and served cold or steamed back to life as in the recipe below, they are excellent. Once you've tried these meaty legs, you will find yourself using them in many different recipes. To go with gumbo, I recommend homemade biscuits, preferably my Black Pepper Biscuits (page 205), or even the ones that come in a can. Just dip and eat. Even Ritz or saltine crackers wouldn't hurt this dinner. A side note: This soup is at its flavor peak when it's a few days old.

Serves 10 to 12

WHAT YOU'LL NEED

Brown Roux

    1 cup (2 sticks) unsalted butter

    1 cup all-purpose flour

Gumbo

    2 tablespoons canola oil

    1½ ounces smoked beef sausages

    1 pound beef hot links, sliced 1 inch thick

    1½ cups diced yellow onion

    1½ cups diced celery

    1 cup diced green bell pepper

    3 cloves garlic, peeled and finely minced

    3 bay leaves

    10 to 12 cups water

    1 to 2 tablespoons filé powder

    Kosher salt and freshly ground pepper to taste

    1 pound chicken wings, washed and cut in half

    1 pound fresh or frozen okra, washed and sliced

    1 28-ounce can diced tomatoes, drained

    1 pound medium shrimp, peeled, deveined, and washed

    2 pounds frozen king crab legs, rinsed and cut into pieces

    8 ounces cooked lump crabmeat

WHAT TO DO FOR THE ROUX

Heat a cast-iron skillet over medium-high heat. Add the butter and melt it. Add the flour and cook, whisking constantly, until the roux is brown but not burnt, 15 to 20 minutes. This thickening agent should be added gradually until your soup reaches desired thickness. Start adding roux to the gumbo broth after the water has reached a medium simmer.

WHAT TO DO FOR THE GUMBO

1. Heat the oil in a large pot over medium-high heat. Add the sausages and hot links and sauté for 6 to 8 minutes. Add the onion, celery, bell pepper, garlic, and bay leaves and cook until the vegetables are softened, 3 to 5 minutes.

2. Add the water to the pot and stir. Bring to a boil, then reduce the heat and simmer. Add half the roux and 1 tablespoon filé powder. Simmer until the gumbo begins to thicken, 35 to 45 minutes.

3. Season the gumbo with salt and pepper to taste. Add the chicken, okra, and tomatoes and continue to simmer for 35 to 40 minutes. Adjust the thickness by adding more roux and filé. If the gumbo becomes too thick, add more water.

4. Add the shrimp and crab legs. Simmer until the shrimp become a little pink and tender, 12 to 15 minutes. Stir in the cooked crabmeat.

5. Serve with steamed rice.

WHAT'S THE STORY

My granddaddy stockpiled the ingredients for this soup (a costly treat for our family) until he had enough shrimp, blue crab, andouille, and hot sausage to make this dish during the holidays. After the big dinner was over, Granddaddy would store the leftovers in mayo jars to serve to visiting relatives. I think he might actually have been proud of my version of King Crab Gumbo with chicken wings and no pork. But I'm sure that if he were still with us, his exact words would be, "Boy, you know you don't put no Alaskan crab and chicken in no gumbo. You been learning that fancy stuff on them jobs." My granddaddy pulled no punches when it came to kitchen tradition.

Grilled Chicken Noodle Soup

The cabbage or collard greens is what sets this classic soup apart from the ordinary version. Using grilled chicken instead of boiled gives the soup a charred taste that makes it memorable. Ritz Crackers or just plain saltines go best here.

Serves 4 to 6

WHAT YOU'LL NEED

6 cups low-sodium chicken broth

2 medium carrots, washed, peeled,
    halved lengthwise, and sliced

1 small yellow onion, peeled and finely diced

16 ounces dried linguini or pasta of choice

½ cup shredded Napa cabbage or cooked
    collard greens

2 cups diced grilled chicken

Kosher salt and freshly ground pepper to taste

WHAT TO DO

1. Bring the broth to a simmer in a medium to large pot. Add the carrots and onion and simmer until half cooked, 6 to 8 minutes.

2. Add the pasta and cook for half of the time recommended on the package, 4 to 6 minutes. Add the cabbage and chicken and simmer for 8 to 10 minutes.

3. Season with salt and pepper to taste. Serve in bowls with crackers.

White Bean Soup and a Sandwich

My sister always made this soup at my mother's request. She used pork neck bones to give it that ultimate flavor, but I make a healthier version with smoked turkey wings. We always ate a fried bologna and cheese sandwich with soup. That sandwich was a family favorite on many nights.

Serves 4 to 8

WHAT YOU'LL NEED

2 tablespoons canola oil

½ yellow onion, peeled and finely chopped

1 stalk celery, washed and finely chopped

2 cloves garlic, peeled and finely minced

2 bay leaves

4 cups low-sodium chicken broth

2 cups dried white or navy beans, soaked
    according to the package

1 smoked small turkey leg or wing

3 tablespoons unsalted butter

Kosher salt and freshly ground pepper to taste

½ cup heavy (whipping) cream

WHAT TO DO

1. Heat the oil in a medium pot over medium-high heat. Add the onion, celery, garlic, and bay leaves and cook until the vegetables are softened.

2. Add the chicken broth, beans, and turkey. If the beans aren't covered, add water until they are. Bring the broth to a boil, then reduce the heat. Simmer until the beans are tender but not mushy, about 2½ hours. The beans should be covered with liquid at all times through the cooking process. Discard the turkey leg after removing the meat. Drain the beans, reserving the cooking liquid.

3. Add half the cooked beans to a blender or food processer, cover with cooking liquid, and puree until smooth. Add butter, season with salt and pepper to taste, and puree. Add half the cream and puree. The soup should not be too thick. Add more cooking liquid if necessary. Repeat the same process for the second batch. Combine batches and serve with turkey meat.

Chef Jeff's Bologna Sandwich

Heat 2 teaspoons unsalted butter in a sauté pan or skillet. Fry either turkey bologna or regular bologna in the butter until it is crispy. Remove the meat from the skillet and place it with a slice of Cheddar cheese between 2 slices of bread. Put the sandwich in the skillet and cook on both sides until the cheese is melted. Remove and serve with white bean soup.

Avocado Soup

This is a cool and refreshing soup for spring and summer. Just put everything in the blender and whip it up. I once made this soup for a fund-raising dinner for the Tavis Smiley Foundation. I put it in shot glasses with a hint of tequila and served it with mini crab cakes. The guests were amazed with the avocado in liquid form. This home version will impress your guests too. Oh, and the tequila is up to you.

Serves 4 to 6

WHAT YOU'LL NEED

3 ripe large avocados

Juice of 1½ limes

1 teaspoon garlic oil (mince 3 cloves garlic
and infuse in ¼ cup olive oil for at
least 30 minutes)

1⅔ cups heavy (whipping) cream,
chilled

⅔ cup sour cream

Handful of ice cubes

1⅔ cups chilled water

2 dashes Tabasco sauce

Kosher salt and freshly ground pepper to taste

1 cup Spicy Chicken Salsa (page 44)

Several sprigs fresh cilantro

WHAT TO DO

1. Halve the avocados and remove the pits. Using a spoon, scoop the flesh into a blender or food processor.

2. Add the lime juice, garlic oil, cream, sour cream, ice, and chilled water. Whip the soup until smooth.

3. Season the puree with Tabasco, salt, and pepper.

4. Pour the soup into bowls or glasses and spoon a little chicken salsa on top.

5. For additional flavor, add a little extra splash of garlic oil to each portion and garnish with the cilantro. Serve immediately.

Corn Chowder

My love of corn goes way back to when I was a kid eating it off the cob or enjoying it cooked in butter with diced red bell pepper. Though corn is always best when it is in season, I still love corn chowder in the winter made with peppers and potatoes—a perfect marriage. You can play with this chunky soup and make it down-home by adding almost any of your favorite vegetables such as cabbage, broccoli, or peas. You can also add chicken, lobster, crab, or shrimp.

Serves 4 to 6

WHAT YOU'LL NEED

5 tablespoons unsalted butter

½ cup finely chopped green bell pepper

½ cup finely chopped yellow onion

3 cloves garlic, peeled and finely minced

2 tablespoons all-purpose flour

1 32-ounce can low-sodium chicken broth

6 ears fresh corn, shucked and corn kernels removed

1¼ cups cubed peeled potatoes

2 bay leaves

1½ cups heavy (whipping) cream

3 tablespoons finely chopped fresh cilantro leaves

1 teaspoon sugar

Kosher salt and freshly ground pepper to taste

WHAT TO DO

1. Heat 2 tablespoons of the butter in a large saucepan over medium-high heat. Add the bell pepper, onion, garlic, and flour and cook until the vegetables are tender, 6 to 8 minutes.

2. Add the chicken broth, corn, potatoes, and bay leaves. Bring to a boil, then reduce the heat. Cover and simmer, stirring occasionally, until the corn and potatoes are tender, 15 to 20 minutes.

3. Add the cream and cilantro and season with the sugar, salt, and pepper. Stir well and let simmer a few more minutes. Corn chowder should be thicker than a soup but not too thick. Serve in a bowl with oyster crackers.

Butternut Squash Soup

When I first came to Gadsby's in the mid-1990s, I'd never seen butternut squash before. Robert Gadsby had many different ways of cooking it, including as a side dish pureed with Vermont maple syrup and in a soup. I came to love this squash and eventually developed my own version by adding the flavors I loved as a child. It's become a favorite at the restaurants where I've been a chef and at home with my family.

Serves 4

WHAT YOU'LL NEED

3 tablespoons unsalted butter

3 tablespoons finely chopped yellow onion

1½ teaspoons grated fresh nutmeg

3 sprigs fresh thyme

2 bay leaves

4 cups cubed peeled butternut squash

1 cup cubed peeled sweet potato

2 cinnamon sticks

5 cups low-sodium chicken broth

1 tablespoon brown sugar

1 cup heavy (whipping) cream

Kosher salt and freshly ground white pepper to taste

½ teaspoon freshly grated nutmeg

WHAT TO DO

1. Melt the butter in a medium pot over medium heat. Add the onion, ginger, thyme, and bay leaves and cook until the onion is tender, 4 to 6 minutes.

2. Add the squash, sweet potato, and cinnamon sticks. Cook, stirring occasionally, until fragrant, 6 to 8 minutes. Pour in the chicken broth, covering the vegetables by about ½ inch. Bring to a boil, then reduce the heat. Simmer until the squash and potato are tender, about 20 minutes.

3. Discard the thyme, bay leaves, and cinnamon sticks. With a slotted spoon, remove the squash and potato. Reserve the cooking liquid.

4. Working in two batches, puree the squash and potato in a blender or food processor, adding the brown sugar and slowly adding the cooking liquid and cream while processing the soup. Season with salt and pepper. Return the soup to the pot and gently reheat.

5. Sprinkle with the nutmeg and serve hot.

Cream of Potato Soup

Serves 4

WHAT YOU'LL NEED

8 tablespoons (1 stick) unsalted butter

1 yellow onion, peeled and finely diced

2 cloves garlic, peeled and finely minced

1 bay leaf

3 cups filtered water

2 cups low-sodium chicken broth

5 cups cubed peeled potatoes

3 to 4 cups heavy (whipping) cream

Kosher salt and freshly ground white pepper to taste

2 chives, finely chopped

WHAT TO DO

1. Melt 2 tablespoons of the butter in a medium pot over medium-high heat. Add the onion, garlic, and bay leaf and let cook until the onion is tender, 6 to 8 minutes.

2. Add the water and broth and bring to a boil. Add the potatoes, reduce the heat, and simmer until the potatoes are tender, 25 to 30 minutes.

3. Discard the bay leaf. Remove the potatoes from the pot with a slotted spoon. Working in two batches, puree the potatoes in a blender or food processor, slowly adding the cooking liquid, cream, and remaining 6 tablespoons butter. Puree the soup until smooth. Season with salt and pepper.

4. Serve in bowls and garnish with chives.

Creamy Plum Tomato Soup

Serves 4 to 6

WHAT YOU'LL NEED

2 tablespoons olive oil

3 cloves garlic, peeled and finely minced

1 medium yellow onion, peeled and finely chopped

2 sprigs fresh thyme

3 tablespoons all-purpose flour

2 cups low-sodium chicken broth

1 28-ounce can whole plum tomatoes,
    pureed with their juice

1½ teaspoons sugar

1 teaspoon dried oregano

Kosher salt and freshly ground pepper to taste

1 cup heavy (whipping) cream

1 cup Italian herbed croutons (available in
    most stores)

3 tablespoons finely chopped fresh basil

¼ cup grated Parmesan cheese

WHAT TO DO

1. Heat the oil in a medium pot over medium heat. Add the garlic, onion, and thyme and cook until the onion is tender, 4 to 6 minutes. Add the flour and stir until thoroughly incorporated.

2. Add the broth, tomatoes, sugar, oregano, and a pinch each of salt and pepper. Bring the soup to a simmer, stirring constantly. Reduce the heat to very low, cover, and gently simmer for 45 to 50 minutes.

3. Taste the soup and season with salt and pepper. Discard the thyme. Puree the soup in several batches, using a blender or food processor and adding cream to each batch while processing.

4. Serve the soup in bowls, topped with croutons, basil, and Parmesan. French bread also accompanies this soup very well.

Chef Robert Gadsby, former chef/owner, Gadsby's, Los Angeles

When Jeff first came to Gadsby's, he was green and I mean green. Everything in our kitchen was new to him. If I said "rough chop the zucchini," he didn't know what rough chop meant; if I asked him to make a mirepoix, he'd never heard the term; if it was time to add the aromatics, he'd no idea what they were. He listened to me about food and the lessons of life because it was a black man talking to him. He was on autopilot back then; he liked to shoot from the hip and didn't stop to analyze what he was doing. I almost had to exorcise the bad habits from him.

It was because of Jeff that I established my rule about the four things that cannot be said in my kitchen: "I know." No you don't. "I've got it." No you haven't. "No problem." There are always problems in a kitchen. "Whatever." No, you will do it this way and only this way!

Eventually Jeff learned that independent thinking and critical analysis are what make you a person. Now he is thinking through ways of expanding on and modernizing these traditional recipes and he's proving that it can be done.

SALADS

As kids we weren't allowed to waste anything, and I still don't. Restaurants don't waste either. You can stretch your food budget by making a healthy salad with leftover meat, chicken, cheese, vegetables, greens, and beans. Now that there are so many great kinds of lettuce on the market, you can use one of them as a base and improvise with the addition of any of these things. But you don't have to have lettuce to put a salad together. Just look around the icebox and make a delicious combination from your leftovers. Dress it with my corn vinaigrette, or blue cheese dressing, or just simple oil and vinegar. I probably make more salads than anything else at home. It's one way that my kids can get all the nutrition they need in a single serving.

Field Greens and Apple Salad

Here's a salad that's similar to the one I used to make at Café Bellagio during the summer. It was so popular there that the pantry ladies who sliced the apples and made the candied walnuts had trouble keeping up with the orders. The tart apples, the sweetness of the walnuts, the rich balsamic vinaigrette, and blue cheese come together in an exciting blend of textures and tastes. You can serve this with any meal in any season, and I know you'll enjoy it as much as the guests at Café Bellagio did.

Serves 4

Creamy Balsamic Vinaigrette (page 101)

½ cup Candied Walnuts (page 50)

20 ounces mixed field greens

½ red onion

2 Granny Smith apples

¾ cup dried cranberries

3½ ounces blue cheese, crumbled

Kosher salt and freshly ground white pepper to taste

WHAT TO DO

1. Prepare the balsamic vinaigrette and the candied walnuts.

2. Wash and thoroughly dry the mixed greens. Refrigerate until ready to serve.

3. Cut the onion into very thin shavings, using a slicer or very sharp knife.

4. Just before serving, cut the apples into wedges. If necessary, hold the apples in water mixed with lime or lemon juice to keep them from browning.

5. To assemble the salad, place the greens, walnuts, cranberries, blue cheese crumbles, red onion, and apples in a medium to large bowl. Toss gently, seasoning with salt and pepper.

6. Add up to 1 cup of the vinaigrette and toss to coat. Arrange the salad on 4 plates and serve immediately.

Crispy Romaine Salad

Serves 4

WHAT YOU'LL NEED

1 package romaine lettuce hearts (18 to 20 ounces)

1 bottle store-bought Caesar salad dressing

Freshly ground pepper to taste

12 saltine crackers

1 ¼- to ½-pound wedge Parmesan cheese

WHAT TO DO

1. Cut the romaine hearts crosswise into 1-inch squares; wash and dry.

2. Toss the lettuce with desire amount of the Caesar dressing in a large bowl. Add pepper to taste.

3. Place the lettuce on individual plates or on a medium platter. Crumble the crackers into bite-size pieces and sprinkle over the lettuce. Shave the Parmesan cheese with a vegetable peeler and lay several sheets on top of the salad. Serve immediately.

My Children's Favorite Fruit Salad

On almost any ramp off the Harbor freeway in Los Angeles you'll encounter a group of migrant farm workers selling the best seasonal fruit from local farms. Stacy and I often stop to buy whatever they have to make a salad for our children. Troy's favorite fruit is seedless watermelon, so this salad of melon, grapes, and berries is a big hit with her.

Serves 4 to 6

WHAT YOU'LL NEED

1 small seedless watermelon, rind removed,
    flesh cut into 1-inch chunks

½ cantaloupe, rind removed, flesh cut into
    1-inch chunks

½ honeydew melon, rind removed, flesh cut into
    1-inch chunks

2 cups strawberries, washed, hulled, and quartered

2 bunches green or red seedless grapes,
    stemmed and washed

1 banana, sliced

1 handful seasonal berries

1 small bunch fresh mint, stems removed,
    leaves thinly sliced

WHAT TO DO

1. After preparing the fruit, keep it refrigerated until ready to serve.
2. Combine all the fruit in a medium bowl and gently toss with some of the mint.
3. Spoon the fruit salad into serving bowls, garnish with the remaining mint, and serve.

Dill Pickle Potato Salad

My wife, Stacy, makes this potato salad, and I will put it up against any other version, including the warm European kind you find on the menus of fine restaurants in Los Angeles and Las Vegas. Stacy's potato salad is easy to make. Just be sure you get the seasoning right, don't forget the pickles, and don't add parsley!

Serves 4 to 6

WHAT YOU'LL NEED

2½ pounds russet potatoes

Kosher salt

3 large eggs

1¼ cups mayonnaise

⅓ cup yellow mustard

1 stalk celery, washed and finely chopped

1½ cups finely diced dill pickles

¼ medium red onion, peeled and finely chopped

Freshly ground pepper to taste

WHAT TO DO

1. Wash and peel the potatoes, then cut them into quarters. Place them in a large pot, cover with water, and add 3 pinches of salt. Bring to a boil, then reduce the heat to medium-high. Cover and boil until the potatoes are fork tender not mushy, 20 to 25 minutes.

2. In another pot, cover the eggs with water and boil for 12 to 14 minutes. Drain the eggs and peel under cold running water. Dry with paper towels and coarsely chop. Set aside.

3. When the potatoes are done, drain and let cool for about 30 minutes. When cool enough to handle, cut into cubes. Place the still-warm potatoes in a large bowl. Fold in

three-quarters of the mayonnaise and mustard and gently mix. Add the eggs, celery, pickles, and onion and gently mix. Taste and adjust the flavor with the remaining mayonnaise and mustard. Season to taste with salt and pepper.

4. Place a lid over the bowl and chill in the refrigerator for at least 4 hours. Serve in individual bowls or on a platter.

West Coast Chopped Salad

This salad is a dinner in itself. You don't have to put fried chicken in it. Smoked turkey, ham, tuna, or even leftover chicken off the bone will also make it memorable. With ingredients like crisp lettuce, avocado, corn, eggs, and blue cheese, you can't go wrong. You can dress it up for guests or dress it down for a family dinner using whatever is in your icebox. I happen to love Friendly Womack's fried chicken strips (page 157) in this salad, but you suit yourself.

Serves 4

WHAT YOU'LL NEED

1 large head romaine lettuce, washed and
    coarsely chopped

2 ripe avocados, peeled, pitted, and diced

3 large eggs, hard boiled, peeled, and
    coarsely chopped

2 small tomatoes, washed, cored, and cut
    into ¼-inch dice

1 cup Grilled Corn on the Cob (page 194)

1 each red and yellow bell peppers, washed,
    seeded, and thinly sliced

3 ounces crumbled blue cheese

12 ounces fried chicken breast, cut into strips

1 cup Buttermilk Dressing (page 97)

Kosher salt and freshly ground pepper to taste

WHAT TO DO

1. Combine the lettuce, avocados, eggs, tomatoes, corn, bell peppers, and blue cheese in a large bowl.

2. When ready to serve, gently toss the chicken with the salad mix. Add the dressing and toss again, seasoning with salt and pepper to taste.

WHAT'S THE STORY

My sister and I didn't have many salads growing up. When we did, the only lettuce we knew was iceberg. My granddaddy would sometimes use iceberg in a salad of cold cuts from Charlie's Kosher Deli in Wilshire, a Westside neighborhood of Los Angeles. At Gadsby's and other fine restaurants, I learned a lot about salads from great chefs. I was soon following their lead in searching out the best ingredients for my creations from the big walk-in refrigerators.

Childhood Iceberg Wedge Salad

This is as simple as salad can get—quick and easy enough to go with any dinner. I love eating this with a T-bone steak. The crisp texture of the lettuce goes well with rich red meat. The creamy blue cheese dressing and ground black pepper just bring this salad home. A must-have with steak!

Serves 4

WHAT YOU'LL NEED

½ head iceberg lettuce, washed, outer layer removed,
    cut into quarters

3 plum tomatoes, washed, cored, and cut into quarters

1 medium English cucumber, washed, peeled, and
    finely diced

½ medium red onion, peeled and thinly sliced

1 teaspoon finely chopped flat-leaf parsley

Creamy Blue Cheese Dressing (page 91)

Kosher salt and freshly ground pepper to taste

WHAT TO DO

Combine the lettuce, tomatoes, and cucumber in a large bowl. Mix in the onion and parsley. Dress with the blue cheese dressing. Season with salt and pepper. Serve right away with seasoned flatbread or crumbled saltine crackers.

WHAT'S THE STORY

Iceberg wedge salads have become a tradition in steak houses. When I was the executive chef at Peter Morton's father's steak house, AJ's at the Hard Rock Hotel in Las Vegas, we served this salad with huge beefsteak tomatoes. Everyone loved it with crumbled blue cheese and buttermilk dressing. Change the dressing to ranch or Thousand Island and it's just as good.

Chef Sarah Bowman, Culinary Consultant

In my many years in the hospitality industry, I have worked with some extraordinary people. These are the ones who stand out either because of their culinary talent or because they have such amazing people skills that a kitchen crew will follow them to the grave. It's rare to find an individual who has both, but then there was Chef Jeff.

Jeff came to help me with a turnover at a hotel where a new company was coming in. We had a stand-up with the kitchen crew to explain everything. Jeff spoke and he was electrifying. He was animated, positive, humble, and respectful. His speech was exactly what the crew needed at the time. He made them feel that they had a home.

Jeff was also relentless in learning about cooking and about the industry. He would not yield. He had a plan and, make no mistake, he has worked for everything he has received, against all odds. He is an inspiration for anyone.

VINAIGRETTES AND DRESSINGS

Salad dressings aren't just for salads. A good vinaigrette also makes a great marinade for meat or chicken, and blue cheese dressing is an ideal dip for wings, chips, salami, and satays. Don't forget that dressings can be drizzled on sandwiches too. When you make a vinaigrette for a salad, you don't have to limit yourself to the traditional ingredients. Add herbs to it, or corn, or garbanzos. Store-bought dressings just can't compare to homemade, as you'll discover when you begin to make your own.

Creamy Blue Cheese Dressing

My creamy blue cheese dressing is simply the best for my Childhood Iceberg Wedge Salad (page 87). It also goes well with buffalo wings or as a dipping sauce served with celery and carrot sticks, or even with ruffled potato chips.

Yields 2 cups

WHAT YOU'LL NEED

¾ cup plain yogurt

¼ cup buttermilk

1 tablespoon vinegar

¼ cup Worcestershire sauce

⅓ cup finely diced red onion

1 tablespoon finely chopped fresh chives

6 tablespoons crumbled blue cheese

Kosher salt and freshly ground pepper to taste

WHAT TO DO

1. Combine the yogurt, buttermilk, vinegar, Worcestershire, and onion in a food processor and pulse until smooth, or whisk with a fork in a bowl.

2. Stir in the chives and blue cheese and season with salt and pepper. Cover and refrigerate until ready to serve.

Avocado Vinaigrette

You'll need a soft, super-ripe Hass avocado (the black one with the pebbly skin) for this simple vinaigrette. A gentle squeeze and if the skin gives a little, you have a ripe one. Plan to make this vinaigrette in the summer when avocados are at their peak of flavor. I use it as a dressing, but I also like it as a sauce with fish.

Yields approximately 3 cups

WHAT YOU'LL NEED

1 avocado, chilled, peeled, pitted, and coarsely
    chopped
⅓ cup finely chopped red onion
2 cups extra-virgin olive oil or avocado oil
½ cup red wine vinegar
3 tablespoons fresh lemon juice
¼ cup finely chopped fresh cilantro leaves
Kosher salt and freshly ground pepper to taste
Dash of Tabasco sauce

WHAT TO DO

Place the avocado, onion, oil, vinegar, lemon juice, and cilantro in a blender and puree until smooth. Season with salt, pepper, and Tabasco. Serve immediately.

Honey-Mustard Dressing

Here's a dressing I made all the time at my first restaurant job. It's best served with a chicken and tomato salad or on a smoked turkey sandwich, a favorite of mine.

Yields approximately 2¼ cups

WHAT YOU'LL NEED

¾ cup pure sweet honey

½ cup Dijon mustard

½ cup mayonnaise

½ cup sour cream

Kosher salt to taste

Several sprigs cilantro, stems removed,
    leaves finely chopped

WHAT TO DO

Whisk the honey, mustard, mayonnaise, and sour cream together in a bowl. Season with salt and correct the seasoning if need be with a couple more teaspoons of honey. Cover and refrigerate until ready to serve. Garnish with cilantro.

WHAT'S THE STORY

This is one of the first fancy dressings I made in my early days of cooking. We would spread it on Italian bread with roast turkey and warm Brie, and once served it at a VIP gala in Watts for Muhammad Ali—a gourmet touch for a meal in the 'hood. Today when I make this sweet honey dressing, I add fresh cilantro, which is a nice touch.

Herb Vinaigrette

This basic vinaigrette is the foundation for many variations. It's also a great marinade for meat or splashed on broiled or grilled fish.

Yields 2 cups

WHAT YOU'LL NEED

½ cup red wine vinegar

1 teaspoon Dijon mustard

¼ red onion, peeled and finely chopped

1 teaspoon finely minced garlic

1½ cups extra-virgin olive oil

3 tablespoons each finely chopped fresh chives,
      parsley, tarragon, and thyme

Pinch of sugar

Kosher salt to taste

¼ teaspoon freshly ground pepper

WHAT TO DO

Place all the ingredients except the sugar, salt, and pepper in a blender and process just enough to incorporate, 8 to 12 seconds. Season with sugar, salt, and pepper. Cover and refrigerate until ready to serve.

Sweet Tomato-Basil Vinaigrette

You can't go wrong tossing a bunch of mixed greens with fresh sweet tomatoes. Just put everything in a blender to make this extremely light vinaigrette. This tomato-based vinaigrette can also be served over grilled vegetables and fresh fish.

Yields 2 cups

WHAT YOU'LL NEED

8 ounces vine-ripened tomatoes, washed,
     seeded, and chopped

1 tablespoon finely chopped red onions

3 cloves garlic, peeled and finely chopped

¼ cup red wine vinegar

½ cup extra-virgin olive oil

1 tablespoon finely chopped fresh basil

1½ teaspoons finely chopped fresh tarragon

2 tablespoons fresh lemon juice

2 tablespoons fresh lime juice

Sugar to taste

Kosher salt and freshly ground white pepper to taste

WHAT TO DO

Place the tomatoes, onion, garlic, vinegar, oil, basil, and tarragon in a blender and process just enough to incorporate, 8 to 12 seconds. Stir in the lemon and lime juices. Season with sugar, salt, and pepper. Cover and refrigerate until ready to serve.

Buttermilk Dressing

This dressing is simple to make. It's another good choice for dipping buffalo wings, potato chips, and crudités.

Yields 2 cups

WHAT YOU'LL NEED

1 cup plain nonfat yogurt

½ cup buttermilk

2 tablespoons fresh lemon juice

2 tablespoons red wine vinegar

2 tablespoons Worcestershire sauce

1 tablespoon Dijon mustard

1 teaspoon finely minced garlic

2 teaspoons finely minced red onion

½ teaspoon celery seeds

1 teaspoon chopped fresh chives

Kosher salt and freshly ground pepper to taste

WHAT TO DO

Place the yogurt, buttermilk, lemon juice, vinegar, Worcestershire, mustard, garlic, onion, and celery seeds in a blender and process on medium speed until all is thoroughly incorporated, 8 to 10 seconds. Pour the buttermilk mixture into a medium bowl, add the chives, and mix lightly with a whisk. Season with salt and pepper to taste. Cover and refrigerate until ready to serve.

Russian Dressing

Yields approximately 2 cups

WHAT YOU'LL NEED

½ cup mayonnaise

½ cup ketchup

¼ cup minced scallions

2 tablespoons capers, drained, rinsed, and
     finely chopped

Freshly ground pepper to taste

Tabasco sauce

WHAT TO DO

Mix the mayonnaise, ketchup, scallions, and capers in a medium bowl. Season with pepper and a dash or two of Tabasco. Cover and refrigerate until ready to serve.

Sweet Corn Vinaigrette

This is a summertime dressing that I like on mixed greens. If you've grilled corn, cut some of the kernels off and add them to the pureed vinaigrette for a little texture.

Yields 2 cups

WHAT YOU'LL NEED

1 cup fresh corn kernels

⅓ red onion, peeled and finely chopped

3 cloves garlic, peeled and finely chopped

½ teaspoon finely minced jalapeño pepper

3 sprigs cilantro, stems removed, leaves finely chopped

¾ cup extra-virgin olive oil

2 tablespoons red wine vinegar

½ teaspoon fresh lime juice

1 teaspoon sugar

Kosher salt and freshly ground white pepper to taste

WHAT TO DO

Place the corn, onion, garlic, jalapeño, cilantro, oil, vinegar, and lime juice in a blender. Process on medium speed until all is fully incorporated, 8 to 10 seconds. Season with sugar, salt, and pepper. Cover and refrigerate until ready to serve.

At the local grocery store buying ingredients for salads and dressings.

Creamy Balsamic Vinaigrette

Here's another salad dressing that is simple to make. This vinaigrette goes well with most lettuces and with poultry or fish. Just put all the ingredients in the blender, pulse, and serve.

Yields 2 cups

WHAT YOU'LL NEED

6 tablespoons best-quality balsamic vinegar

1½ cups extra-virgin olive oil

2 teaspoons Dijon mustard

2 garlic cloves, peeled and finely minced

2 tablespoons minced red onion

1 teaspoon finely minced fresh thyme leaves

Pinch of light brown sugar

Kosher salt and freshly ground white pepper to taste

WHAT TO DO

Place all the ingredients except the sugar, salt, and pepper in a blender and process on medium speed until fully blended, 8 to 10 seconds. Season with sugar, salt, and pepper. Cover and refrigerate until ready to serve.

Citrus-Orange Vinaigrette

This dressing goes well with any mixed greens and is even better drizzled on segments of whatever citrus fruit you used to make the vinaigrette. When blood oranges are in season, adding a bit of their juice and a little of their zest really makes this vinaigrette stand out.

Yields approximately 1 cup

WHAT YOU'LL NEED

½ cup extra-virgin olive oil

¼ cup freshly squeezed orange juice

3 tablespoons best-quality balsamic vinegar

1 teaspoon Dijon mustard

¼ red onion, peeled and minced

2 cloves garlic, peeled and finely minced

Several sprigs fresh thyme, stems removed,
    leaves finely chopped

Kosher salt and freshly ground pepper to taste

WHAT TO DO

Place the oil, orange juice, vinegar, mustard, onion, garlic, and thyme in a blender. Process on medium speed until all is fully incorporated, 8 to 10 seconds. Season with salt and pepper. Cover and refrigerate until ready to serve.

FAMILY-STYLE SANDWICHES

Growing up we had fried bologna sandwiches, peanut butter and jelly sandwiches, and sandwiches made from government-issued cheese that was so hard it would hurt your hand trying to cut it. I make several kinds of sandwiches for my family now, though I'll admit that my kids also look forward to the ones they get at Subway. Like salads, sandwiches are a way of getting all your nutrition in one place. A really good one with a lot of different textures and flavors is like a package with a great surprise inside. I do have one rule about the sandwich I make for myself: It must have pickles in it if I'm going to enjoy it. Peanut butter and jelly is the obvious exception, but all the rest MUST HAVE PICKLES!

"Big and Easy" Oyster Po' Boy

Oyster po' boys were a special treat at my grandparents' home as far back as I can remember. My granddaddy, it goes without saying, sometimes added fried shrimp to them. They're great served with potato salad or just plain potato chips. Don't forget to test one oyster first before you fry up a whole batch to make sure you have the flavor and texture you want just right.

Serves 4

WHAT YOU'LL NEED

4 cups canola oil

1 cup all-purpose flour

½ cup yellow cornmeal

1 teaspoon cayenne pepper

Kosher salt and freshly ground pepper to taste

3 large eggs

⅓ cup whole milk

3 dozen medium to large oysters, shucked and
    drained

1 20-inch loaf soft French or Italian bread, split
    lengthwise and hollowed out slightly

2 tablespoons mayonnaise

1 teaspoon Tabasco sauce

¼ head iceberg lettuce, washed and shredded

2 tomatoes, washed, cored, and thinly sliced

1 large dill pickle, thinly sliced

WHAT TO DO

1. Heat the oil in a deep skillet to 350 degrees. (The skillet should be deep enough that the oil fills it between one-third and one-half full and does *not* bubble over the top while the food is frying.)

2. Mix the flour, cornmeal, cayenne, and ½ teaspoon each salt and pepper in a medium bowl.

3. Beat the eggs and milk together in a small to medium bowl.

4. Rinse the oysters well under cold running water. Spread the oysters on a platter lined with paper towels and season with salt and pepper.

5. Dip the seasoned oysters into the egg wash, then coat them with the flour mixture. Place coated oysters on dry paper towels.

6. Deep-fry one oyster to test for cooking temperature and flavor adjustments. Make necessary changes if need be.

7. Deep-fry the oysters in batches until golden and cooked through. Drain on paper towels.

8. To make the sandwiches, mix the mayonnaise and Tabasco and spread each side of the bread with the spicy mayonnaise. Layer the lettuce, tomatoes, and dill pickle on the bread and top with the fried oysters. Close the po' boy, cut into quarters, and serve at once.

Roasted Portobello Sandwich

This is a great sandwich because it's both healthy and light. I've served one like it at several restaurants that I've worked in. The textures of the romaine lettuce, tomatoes, and melted provolone go well with the charred, roasted, herb-marinated mushrooms. This is an easy dish to make at home. Serve it with beer and chips.

Serves 4

WHAT YOU'LL NEED

4 tablespoons extra-virgin olive oil

3 tablespoons balsamic vinegar

1 clove garlic, peeled and finely chopped

Several sprigs fresh rosemary, stems removed, leaves finely chopped

Kosher salt and freshly ground pepper to taste

8 large portobello mushrooms

4 kaiser rolls, split

Dijon mustard to taste

8 slices provolone cheese

1 medium head butter lettuce, cored, washed, and leaves separated

3 ripe large tomatoes, washed, cored, and thinly sliced

WHAT TO DO

1. Preheat the oven to 350 degrees. Mix 3 tablespoons of the oil, the vinegar, garlic, rosemary, and a pinch each of salt and pepper in a medium bowl.

2. Rinse the mushrooms and pat dry. Remove the stems by applying a little pressure with your hand. Add the mushrooms to the oil mixture and turn to coat.

3. Place the mushrooms, stem side down, in 1 or 2 baking dishes just large enough to hold them. Sprinkle with a pinch or two salt and pepper.

4. Cover the baking dish tightly with plastic wrap and then aluminum foil. Bake for 15 to 20 minutes. Remove the foil, puncture the plastic to allow the steam to escape, and remove the plastic.

5. Heat the remaining 1 tablespoon oil in a medium skillet over medium heat. Place the rolls, cut side down, in the skillet and cook until toasted, 2 to 4 minutes.

6. To assemble the sandwiches, spread mustard on one side of one roll. Place 2 whole mushrooms on the other side. Cover the mushrooms with lettuce and tomato and top with the other half of the roll. Repeat the process for additional sandwiches. Serve immediately.

Roast Turkey Sandwich

From the school cafeteria to leftover turkey sandwiches after Thanksgiving dinner, you just can't go wrong. Any time and any place, these sandwiches are terrific. Turkey comes prepared many different ways, but this recipe calls for roast turkey, my favorite.

Serves 4 to 6

WHAT YOU'LL NEED

¼ cup Dijon mustard

¼ teaspoon honey

4 to 6 crusty hoagie rolls or small French baguettes

1½ pounds roast turkey breast, sliced

2 large tomatoes, washed and thinly sliced

1 large dill pickle, thinly sliced

½ head butter lettuce, washed and leaves separated

8 slices Swiss cheese

WHAT TO DO

1. Mix the mustard and honey in a small bowl.
2. Cut the rolls in half lengthwise and place on a platter.
3. To assemble the sandwiches, spread the sweet mustard over both halves of the rolls. Place the slices of turkey on one side and follow with the tomatoes, pickle, lettuce, and cheese. Top with the other half of the roll. Serve immediately with soup or chips.

Roasted Portobello Sandwich (108)

King Crab Gumbo (61)

Marbled Sweet Potato Cheesecake (225)

"Big and Easy" Oyster Po' Boy (105)

Ground Beef Tacos (174)

Sunday Morning Cinnamon Rolls (207)

Herb Vinaigrette (94)

Honey-Mustard Dressing (93)

Sweet Corn Vinaigrette (99)

Creamy Balsamic Vinaigrette (101)

Molasses Braised Beef Short Ribs (176)
with Buttermilk Mashed Potatoes (148)

Spicy Cilantro Pesto (41)

Sweet Tomato-Basil Vinaigrette (95)

Creamy Blue Cheese Dressing (91)

Chunky Peanut Sauce (43)

Avocado Vinaigrette (92)

Sautéed Carrots (126)

Sautéed Garlicky
Spinach (130)

Back-in-the-Day
Creamed Corn (39)

Mashed Butternut
Squash (150)

Sautéed Striped Sea Bass (170)

Friendly Fried Chicken (157) and
Buttermilk Waffles (211)

Marinated Watermelon Cubes (16)
and Crispy Crab Cakes (13)

Chocolate S'more Bread Pudding (221)

Indoor Barbecue Chicken Sandwich

Chicken goes well with almost any type of sauce and can be paired with most starches and vegetables. This sandwich calls for my homemade barbecue sauce, but you can buy your favorite store brand and make it with that. Oh! Don't forget my easy-to-make Cole Slaw (page 46) to go with it.

Serves 4 to 6

WHAT YOU'LL NEED

6 boneless, skinless chicken breast halves
(about 8 ounces each)
Kosher salt and freshly ground pepper to taste
¼ cup canola oil
1½ cups Smoked Molasses Barbecue Sauce
(page 42)
¼ head Iceberg lettuce, washed and leaves separated
4 to 6 whole-wheat burger buns
8 slices smoked Cheddar cheese
2 large tomatoes, washed and thinly sliced
1 large dill pickle, thinly sliced

WHAT TO DO

1. Preheat the oven to 350 degrees. Season the chicken breasts with salt and pepper well and evenly.

2. Heat the oil in a large sauté pan over medium-high heat. Add the chicken and sear for about 3 minutes on each side until crispy brown. Place the pan in the oven and bake until the chicken is tender and juicy, 12 to 15 minutes.

3. Bring the barbecue sauce to a simmer in a small pan, then pour it into a large bowl.

4. Remove the chicken from the oven and drain off any cooking oil. Place the chicken breasts in the barbecue sauce and turn to coat the chicken well.

5. To assemble the sandwiches, place 2 lettuce leaves on one half of each bun, then add 1 chicken breast. Add the cheese, tomatoes, and pickle and cover with the other half of the bun. Serve immediately.

Half-pound "Back-in-the-Day" Chili Cheeseburger

This burger was inspired by the legendary Los Angeles Fat Burger on Western Avenue. I just reworked it by adding onions, fresh garlic, and bell peppers to the meat. It's just as good as the original, and you'll still need a bib and plenty of napkins. This burger goes well with homemade fries and a bottle of Pineapple Crush Soda.

Serves 4

WHAT YOU'LL NEED

2 pounds ground beef

½ yellow onion, peeled and finely diced

½ green bell pepper, washed, seeded, and
     finely diced

3 cloves garlic, peeled and finely chopped

⅓ cup A-1 steak sauce

Kosher salt and freshly ground pepper to taste

4 slices Cheddar cheese

Yellow mustard to taste

4 medium to large hamburger buns

Mayonnaise to taste

1⅓ cups Spicy Turkey Chili (page 33), warm

2 large tomatoes, washed and sliced

1 large dill pickle, thinly sliced

¼ head iceberg lettuce, washed and leaves
     separated

WHAT TO DO

1. Heat a large cast-iron skillet over medium heat. Place the ground beef, onion, bell pepper, garlic, and steak sauce in a large bowl. Gently mix the ingredients together, seasoning the meat mixture with salt and pepper.

2. On a piece of plastic wrap, shape the burger meat into patties. Pack them tightly with your hands to keep them from coming apart while cooking.

3. Lightly season the burgers on both sides with salt and pepper. Place the burgers in the skillet over medium heat and cook for 3 to 4 minutes. Flip the burgers and continue to cook 3 to 4 minutes on the other side or to desired doneness. Top each burger with 1 slice of cheese and continue to cook until the cheese has melted.

4. Spread mustard on the bottom of each bun and mayonnaise on the top. Place the buns on a platter and a burger on the bottom of each bun. Spoon chili on top of the burgers and top with tomatoes, pickle, and lettuce. Cover with the top half of the bun. Serve immediately.

Pastrami Sandwich

I would take a pastrami sandwich over a Reuben sandwich any day. Flavored pastrami with melted Swiss cheese and sliced pickle is an unbeatable combination. When I was growing up in Los Angeles, Johnny's Pastrami was the greatest pastrami joint on the West Coast. It's my inspiration for this version, which is simple to make. Add extra pickles!

Serves 4

WHAT YOU'LL NEED

4 tablespoons unsalted butter

1½ pounds cooked pastrami, thinly sliced

4 6-inch French bread loaves

¼ cup yellow mustard

⅓ cup mayonnaise

8 slices Swiss cheese

2 large dill pickles, sliced

WHAT TO DO

1. Heat a large sauté pan over medium-high heat. Add the butter and melt it. Add the pastrami and cook until it is very hot, 6 to 8 minutes.

2. Cut the loaves of bread in half lengthwise. Spread mustard on the bottom halves of bread and mayonnaise on the top halves.

3. Arrange the pastrami on the bread bottoms, add the cheese and pickles, and cover with the bread tops. Serve immediately.

White Albacore Tuna Sandwich

Serves 4

WHAT YOU'LL NEED

1 12-ounce can white albacore tuna

3 large eggs, hard boiled, shelled, and chopped

1 cup mayonnaise

1 tablespoon Dijon mustard

¼ red onion, peeled and finely diced

1 tablespoon finely diced dill pickle

Kosher salt and freshly ground pepper to taste

8 slices whole-wheat bread

½ head iceberg lettuce, washed and leaves separated

1 ripe large tomato, washed, cored, and thinly sliced

4 slices Cheddar cheese

WHAT TO DO

1. Drain the tuna thoroughly.

2. Place the tuna, eggs, mayonnaise, mustard, onion, and pickle in a medium bowl and gently mix together. Season with salt and pepper to taste.

3. Spread the tuna mixture on 4 slices of the bread and top with the lettuce, tomato, and a slice of cheese. Cover with the remaining slices of bread. Serve immediately with chips.

The Hotel Bel-Air

With a growing family I eventually realized that I needed health insurance and a better income, so I decided to look for a job in a hotel restaurant. Most small restaurants didn't offer medical insurance, and they couldn't pay you well enough to support a family. Hotel restaurants were less competitive, had less talented cooks, and had a lot of corporate rules to follow, but when I went to Marriott I earned $10.00 an hour for the first time. Robert Gadsby didn't encourage me when I expressed the wish to work in a hotel restaurant. He thought they required you to cook for too many people and had too many restrictions on quality ingredients. But later he helped me anyway by taking me to the exclusive Hotel Bel-Air for an interview with its executive chef, Gary Clauson. I'd never heard of the Bel-Air, so I didn't know what a huge deal this was. Robert talked me up to Clauson, maybe a little too much. When I looked in the kitchen and saw the action there with all those cooks grinding away, I was intimidated. Could I deliver?

The Bel-Air was where I really learned to expedite. You had to be totally focused there; if you missed a beat, you could crash the whole kitchen. There was no room for talking or messing around. It was all about speed, focus, and organization. Clauson was like a general calling out orders, and you had to remember them because there were no tickets for the cooks to see. When he called out "Henderson all day," he was about to give me a full rundown of all my orders. When his voice got really loud, I started getting nervous and my stomach would be in an uproar. I worked every station at the Bel-Air, and in the beginning I often used my break to call Robert with questions about stuff I didn't understand. Among other things, I was intimidated by the wide range of wines and liquor. I don't drink and all this was baffling to me.

Clauson's food was classic European with a lot of sauces all made from scratch. That's where Mario, the master of sauces, came in. Mario was a chubby Mexican guy with a bit of a stomach that he liked to rest on the plating board. He'd keep sixteen sauces lined up on the stove with the pot handles all facing one way, each one labeled with a piece of duct tape. Mario was the leader in the kitchen, and he brokered the peace for me until the crew finally accepted me. I worked hard for Mario because I wanted to be in with the crew and to learn his sauces.

As I said, the pressure was intense. It was like running downcourt in a basketball game with every player aware of what every other player is doing. If you screwed up, everyone paid the price. And sometimes we did screw up, but there was something interesting about that. However well or badly things went, Chef Clauson always came by at the end of the night to say "Good night, great job."

By the time I became banquet chef at the Bel-Air, I had adopted Clauson's motivational technique. Thanking people is the right thing to do, but thanking people is also just good sense. It keeps guys from doing things like calling in sick just before a big event or taking another job for a few pennies more. This taught me the value of recognizing the efforts of the crew and the cooks; it's a practice I employed when I became a chef myself. Every night at the Bellagio, I thanked my cooks. I know they went home feeling good about themselves just as I had when Gary recognized me for my good work.

VEGETABLES AND GREENS

My wife and I always buy fresh vegetables for our family, and when I cook them, I don't dress them up too much. Fresh vegetables just don't need it. As kids we had canned vegetables for the most part, and they do benefit from a little creativity with the addition of onions, spices and a dash of sugar. But with fresh vegetables, why try to improve on a good thing? You can blanch your vegetables in the morning and plunge them in ice water to stop the cooking before draining and refrigerating them. That way they'll be ready for you when you need them in the evening. Just take them from the fridge and cook briefly. I like vegetables with a little crunch to them—not too raw and definitely not mushy. But what if you do overcook them? Just put them in the blender with broth, cream, and butter and puree until you have a soup. For the creative cook, almost nothing is lost.

Turkey Smoked Collard Greens

Collard greens are traditionally cooked with ham hocks, but I make them with smoked turkey legs or wings and low-sodium chicken broth. This is a healthier version and every bit as good. I'm sure you know what these greens go with—chicken, beans and rice, and my Cakelike Cornbread (page 199).

Serves 6 to 8

WHAT YOU'LL NEED

8 cups low-sodium chicken broth

2½ pounds smoked turkey wings

1 large yellow onion, peeled and thinly sliced

2 bunches fresh collard greens, washed,
     stems removed, leaves cut into bite-size pieces

1 tablespoon distilled white vinegar

4 tablespoons unsalted butter

2 teaspoons sugar

Kosher salt and freshly ground white pepper to taste

WHAT TO DO

1. Bring the chicken broth to a slow boil in a large pot over medium heat. Add the turkey, onion, collard greens, and vinegar.

2. Let the greens cook for a few minutes, then cover the pot and turn the heat down to low. Simmer until the greens are tender, about 1½ hours. Add the butter and sugar and season with salt and white pepper.

3. Serve with a slotted spoon.

Grilled Asparagus

Serves 6

WHAT YOU'LL NEED

2 pounds asparagus, bottoms trimmed

1 tablespoon finely minced garlic

2 tablespoons extra-virgin olive oil

Kosher salt and freshly ground pepper to taste

WHAT TO DO

1. Set up a grill for direct cooking over medium heat and oil the grate with canola oil or cooking spray.

2. Place the asparagus in a medium baking pan. Add the garlic and oil, season with salt and pepper, and toss to coat.

3. Place the asparagus directly on the grill or in a grill basket. Grill until just tender and lightly charred, about 5 minutes.

Sautéed Carrots

Serves 4 to 6

WHAT YOU'LL NEED

2 tablespoons canola oil

8 medium carrots, peeled and cut into 2-inch rounds

Several sprigs flat-leaf parsley, stems removed,
     leaves finely chopped

2 tablespoons sugar

Kosher salt and freshly ground pepper to taste

4 tablespoons unsalted butter

Enough chicken broth or water to cover the carrots

WHAT TO DO

Heat the oil in a large skillet over medium heat. Add the carrots, parsley, sugar, and a pinch each of salt and pepper. Cook, turning the carrots every few minutes, until they begin to soften, about 5 minutes. Add the butter, reduce the heat to medium-low, and add enough broth or water to almost cover the carrots. Cook, turning the carrots frequently, until they are tender, 12 to 15 minutes more.

Sautéed String Beans

Most folks cook string beans by boiling them until tender and then sautéing them quickly with bacon, onions, and a little butter. Here's a healthier version of that recipe.

Serves 4

WHAT YOU'LL NEED

Kosher salt

1 pound string beans, trimmed and washed

6 tablespoons extra-virgin olive oil

½ medium onion, peeled and thinly sliced

2 cloves garlic, peeled and finely minced

3 tablespoons unsalted butter

Freshly ground pepper to taste

WHAT TO DO

1. Add water to a medium pot and bring to a boil. Salt the water and add the beans. Boil until cooked through but still a little crunchy, 10 to 12 minutes.

2. Remove the beans from the boiling water with a slotted spoon and add to a medium bowl filled with ice water to stop the cooking process. Drain and shake off excess water.

3. Heat the oil and butter in a large skillet over medium heat. Add the beans, onion, and garlic and sauté until the beans are tender. Season with pepper to taste. Serve immediately.

Caramelized Cabbage

Almost everyone is familiar with either Savoy or Napa cabbage. Each lends itself to a wide variety of recipes. My granddaddy used to stuff cabbage with meat and rice, and I've often made beef and cabbage soup. But my favorite way of making cabbage is simply to blanch it and then caramelize it in butter. Serve it with your favorite meat.

Serves 4

WHAT YOU'LL NEED

Kosher salt

1½ heads Savoy cabbage, outer leaves removed, cut into ½-inch-wide strips

3 tablespoons unsalted butter

Freshly ground pepper to taste

WHAT TO DO

1. Fill a medium pot three-quarters full with water and bring it to a boil. Salt the water, add the cabbage, and boil for about 8 minutes. Remove the cabbage from the water with a slotted spoon. The cabbage should be undercooked and a bit crunchy.

2. Place the cabbage in a bowl of ice water to cool it. Once the cabbage is cooled, drain it well.

3. Melt the butter in a medium skillet over medium heat. Add the cabbage and sauté until the cabbage is caramelized and turning just a bit brown on the edges, 8 to 12 minutes. Remove from the pan. Season to taste with salt and pepper and serve at once.

Sautéed Garlicky Spinach

At Café Bellagio we served spinach many different ways. Our guests liked it raw in salads with toasted pine nuts, or creamed as a side dish, and, yes, even as spinach soup. But most orders were for spinach sautéed with fresh garlic and seasoned with salt and pepper—something I still enjoy cooking and eating.

Serves 4 to 6

WHAT YOU'LL NEED

4 tablespoons extra-virgin olive oil

3 cloves garlic, peeled and finely chopped

1½ pounds spinach, washed and stems removed

Kosher salt and freshly ground pepper to taste

WHAT TO DO

Heat the oil in a large skillet over medium-high heat. Stir in the garlic and cook quickly for about 15 seconds. Add the spinach and quickly toss to coat. Season to taste with salt and pepper and serve immediately.

Broccoli with Cheddar Sauce

Serves 4 to 6

WHAT YOU'LL NEED

¾ cup (1½ sticks) unsalted butter

½ cup all-purpose flour

2 teaspoons kosher salt, plus additional to taste

¼ teaspoon cayenne pepper

5½ cups whole milk

1 cup grated sharp Cheddar cheese

Freshly ground pepper to taste

1½ pounds broccoli, stems trimmed, cut into large florets

WHAT TO DO

1. Melt ½ cup of the butter in a heavy medium saucepan over medium heat. Add the flour and whisk constantly until thickened to a golden brown roux, 6 to 8 minutes. Add 2 teaspoons salt and the cayenne and stir well. Gradually whisk in the milk and cook, whisking constantly, until thickened, 4 to 6 minutes.

2. Add the cheese and cook, whisking constantly, until the cheese is melted. Remove from the heat. Set aside.

3. Bring a medium pot of salted water to a boil. Add the broccoli and remaining ¼ cup butter. Cook until the broccoli is tender but still a little firm, 8 to 10 minutes. Drain the broccoli in a colander and place in a bowl. Gently fold in the hot cheese sauce and serve.

On My Own

There came a time after my work with Robert Gadsby, Sarah Bowman, and Gary Clauson that I wanted to take what I'd learned and go out on my own, so I started a catering company called Posh Urban Cuisine and set out to get some work from the African American community. Eventually radio and TV host Tavis Smiley's office called and asked me to do a fund-raiser for his Los Angeles organization called Salute to Youth Leadership. They held these events annually in a celebrity's home, and the food was always catered by a well-known African American chef. When my turn came, I was determined to blow them away and establish my brand.

I scouted the layout of the Larkin mansion in Bel Air where the Salute to Youth event was to take place, and I planned everything down to the last detail. It was a huge event with seventy-five members of the city's black elite, everyone from Congresswoman Maxine Waters to L.A.'s police chief Barnard Parks and other celebrities.

The evening went off almost perfectly. My crew was ready and we executed like pros. We amazed everyone and here's why: I knew how to appeal to the African American palate. I knew how to take them down-home with every dish, so that if I served something elegant like roasted quail, it had a cornbread and cabbage stuffing; my upscale crab cake came with avocado and barbecued crème fraîche; the sweet corn soup had butter-poached lobster tail and collards in it. See what I mean? Everything high-end had a taste of the South somewhere.

My success that evening led to other events—one for *Black Enterprise* magazine's Hot List, another for the seventy-fifth anniversary of the NAACP, a dinner to honor Mario Van Peebles, and so forth. But that isn't really the point. This is: That first evening was a shining moment in my life as a chef. It was the first time when everyone could see that I was more than an ex-con with a story about falling into crime and rising up again. I was on my own with my people, using my own instincts and cooking my own food.

Oh, and one more thing. My wife, Stacy, and my parents came to that dinner and stood in the kitchen watching me. My mom couldn't believe it was her son that all these people were admiring and praising. My dad got the whole thing down in photographs.

At this point in my life, my confidence is high and my vision clear.

POTATOES, STARCHES, AND GRAINS

Nowadays people are wary of starches but I don't think they need to be. Just balance the starches with protein and vegetables, and you won't have to worry about your health. Most starches taste just as good or better the day after they are made. You can put leftover mashed potatoes in the blender with chicken broth, a little cream, and some salt and pepper and you'll have a good potato soup. Leftover rice and leftover beans can be brought back to life with a little broth. Remember, your freezer is your friend here. Many starches freeze well and are great to have on hand.

Sweet Potato Risotto

You can add a lot of different ingredients to a basic risotto, from meat and shellfish to any number of vegetables. I've added caramelized cubes of sweet potato here to give this traditional Italian dish a down-home taste.

Serves 4 to 6

WHAT YOU'LL NEED

6 to 8 cups low-sodium chicken broth

3 tablespoons unsalted butter

1 large sweet potato or yam, washed, peeled,
    and cut into ½-inch dice

2 tablespoons (packed) light brown sugar

1 teaspoon ground cinnamon

½ teaspoon freshly grated nutmeg

6 tablespoons extra-virgin olive oil

1 small onion, peeled and finely chopped

1 tablespoon finely chopped fresh sage

1½ teaspoons peeled and finely minced garlic

4 sprigs fresh thyme

1½ cups Arborio (risotto) rice

¾ cup dry white wine

¾ cup grated Parmesan, or as needed

Kosher salt and freshly ground pepper to taste

WHAT TO DO

1. Pour the chicken broth into a medium saucepan and bring to a boil. Reduce the heat and let it simmer.

2. Melt the butter in a medium sauté pan over medium heat. Add the sweet potato, brown sugar, cinnamon, and nutmeg. Gently cook the potato just until fork tender. Don't overcook it.

3. Heat the oil in a medium pot over medium-high heat. Add the onion, garlic, sage, and thyme and cook for 5 to 6 minutes. Add the rice and continue to cook, stirring constantly, for 7 to 10 minutes. Add the wine and stir until it is absorbed. Add the chicken broth, 1 cup at a time, stirring and cooking until it is absorbed before adding another cup of broth. Continue until the rice is thoroughly cooked, 12 to 15 minutes. Add the Parmesan cheese and remove from the heat. Stir in the sweet potato and season with salt and pepper.

4. Serve in individual bowls or family style in a large bowl.

Potatoes and Caramelized Onions

My granddaddy always cooked potatoes and fried onions to go with his smothered liver. I never ate the liver, but the texture and flavor of the caramelized potatoes and onions was something I loved and still make. When I cooked at the Ritz Carlton, the French chefs called them Lyonnaise potatoes. I really enjoy them with a steak and A-1 steak sauce.

Serves 4

WHAT YOU'LL NEED

¼ cup canola oil

1 large Vidalia onion, peeled, halved, and thinly sliced

Kosher salt and freshly ground pepper to taste

4 tablespoons unsalted butter

6 large russet potatoes, washed, peeled, and
sliced ⅓ inch thick

Several sprigs flat-leaf parsley, stems removed,
leaves finely chopped

WHAT TO DO

1. Heat the oil in a large sauté pan over medium-high heat.

2. Add the onion, season with salt and pepper, and cook until caramelized (the onion will soften and brown), 15 to 20 minutes. Remove from the heat and set aside.

3. Melt the butter in a second large sauté pan over medium heat. Add the potatoes and cook, turning gently, until tender and crispy brown, 12 to 15 minutes. Add the onion to the potatoes and adjust the seasoning with salt and pepper. Add the parsley and gently mix. Serve hot.

Dirty Rice with Turkey

Dirty rice is the American South's version of Asian fried rice. This version is not cooked in a wok; it is best cooked in a cast-iron skillet. I do use turkey and not the traditional chicken gizzards. This dish can be served as a side dish or main course.

Serves 4 to 6

WHAT YOU'LL NEED

2 cups long-grain white rice, rinsed

4 cups low-sodium chicken broth

Kosher salt

2 tablespoons canola oil

4 cloves garlic, peeled and finely minced

1 cup finely diced yellow onion

¾ cup finely diced green bell pepper

8 ounces ground turkey

1 bay leaf

¼ teaspoon cayenne pepper

Freshly ground pepper to taste

1 bunch scallions (tops only),
    washed and finely chopped

WHAT TO DO

1. Soak the rice in water for about 30 minutes to allow any impurities to float to the top. Drain. Place the rice in a pot and add the chicken broth and a pinch of salt. Bring to a boil, then reduce the heat. Cover and simmer for 20 minutes.

2. Heat the oil in a large sauté pan over medium heat. Add the garlic, onion, and bell pepper and cook until softened, 6 to 8 minutes. Add the ground turkey and bay leaf and cook until the turkey is browned, 10 to 12 minutes. Season with the cayenne and salt and pepper to taste.

3. Add the rice and scallion tops to the meat mixture and cook, stirring constantly, over low heat for 12 to 15 minutes. Adjust the seasoning, remove the bay leaf, and serve hot.

Macaroni and Smoked Cheddar Cheese

There are a lot of different versions of macaroni and cheese. My take on this favorite has great visual appeal due to the use of three kinds of Cheddar cheese—sharp yellow, mild white, and mild smoked. It's the smoked Cheddar that really enhances this longtime favorite.

Serves 6 to 8

WHAT YOU'LL NEED

3 tablespoons canola oil

4 cups elbow macaroni

4 tablespoons unsalted butter, softened

1 cup grated mild white Cheddar cheese

1½ cups grated mild smoked Cheddar cheese

1½ cups grated sharp yellow Cheddar cheese

1 tablespoon kosher salt

1 tablespoon freshly ground pepper

2 cups milk

WHAT TO DO

1. Preheat the oven to 350 degrees.

2. Drizzle the oil into a large pot of boiling salted water. Add the pasta and cook according to the directions on the package. Drain well.

3. Transfer the noodles to a large stainless steel bowl, add the butter, and mix well. Add the cheeses, reserving ½ cup of the smoked and yellow Cheddar cheeses for the topping. Add the salt and pepper and stir well. Stir in the milk and adjust the seasoning.

4. Transfer the noodle mixture to a 13- by 9-inch baking dish or individual baking dishes, cover with aluminum foil, and bake for 25 to 35 minutes. Sprinkle with the reserved cheeses and bake, uncovered, until all the cheese is melted, 15 to 20 minutes more. Serve immediately.

Candied Yams

With yams or sweet potatoes, the whole point comes down to the sauce. This dish is best made from scratch, but if you master the sauce, you can make a pretty mean version using canned yams or canned sweet potatoes.

Serves 4 to 6

WHAT YOU'LL NEED

4 medium yams or sweet potatoes, washed, peeled, and sliced ¼ inch thick

2 tablespoons light brown sugar

2¼ teaspoons freshly grated nutmeg

1½ teaspoons ground cinnamon

1 teaspoon pure vanilla extract

4 tablespoons unsalted butter

Candied Yam Sauce (recipe follows)

WHAT TO DO

1. Preheat the oven to 350 degrees.

2. Bring salted water to a boil in a medium pot. Add the yams and boil until three-quarters done, about 20 minutes. The yams should not be fork tender.

3. Gently remove the yams from the pot with a slotted spoon and reserve 2¼ cups of the cooking liquid for the sauce (see below). Layer the yams in an ovenproof baking dish and sprinkle with the brown sugar, nutmeg, cinnamon, and vanilla extract. Dot with the butter. Cover with aluminum foil and bake for 25 to 30 minutes.

4. Pour the candied yam sauce over the baked yams. Cover with foil and bake for 12 to 15 minutes.

5. Remove the candied yams from the oven. Let sit for 15 to 20 minutes before serving.

Candied Yam Sauce

This sauce is the key to this recipe; keep stirring and tasting until it begins to taste like candy. You should start making this sauce as soon as you start baking your yams.

WHAT YOU'LL NEED

2¼ cups reserved cooking liquid

1 cup (packed) light brown sugar

1 teaspoon ground cinnamon

½ teaspoon freshly grated nutmeg

1 teaspoon pure vanilla extract

3 tablespoons all-purpose flour

WHAT TO DO

1. Pour 2 cups of the cooking liquid into a medium pot and bring to a slow boil. Add the brown sugar, cinnamon, nutmeg, and vanilla and whisk together well. Reduce the heat and simmer.

2. Whisk the flour and remaining ¼ cup cooking liquid together in a small bowl. Add the flour mixture to the pot and cook, whisking constantly, until thickened, 5 to 8 minutes.

Big Easy Red Beans and Rice

The red beans in this dish are traditionally cooked with a ham hock, but I've substituted a smoked turkey leg for the pork. You get great flavor and a healthier dish. You can also add cooked ground beef to turn this from a side dish into a hearty meal.

Serves 8 to 12

WHAT YOU'LL NEED

1 pound dried red kidney beans

2 tablespoons unsalted butter

4 garlic cloves, peeled and finely minced

2 bay leaves

5 sprigs fresh thyme

1 cup finely diced yellow onion

½ cup finely diced green bell pepper

½ cup finely diced celery

3 tablespoons all-purpose flour

1 pound smoked turkey leg or wing

4 to 5 cups low-sodium chicken broth

Kosher salt and freshly ground pepper to taste

3 cups long-grain rice, cooked

WHAT TO DO

1. Soak the beans in water to cover for at least 24 hours, then drain.

2. Melt the butter in a large heavy pot over medium heat. Add the garlic, bay leaves, thyme, onion, bell pepper, celery, and flour. Cook, stirring frequently, until the vegetables are tender, 10 to 12 minutes.

3. Add the beans and smoked turkey and stir well. Add enough chicken broth to cover the beans. Bring to a boil, then reduce the heat to low and cover the pot. Simmer, stirring occasionally, until the beans are tender, 2 to 2½ hours. Season to taste with salt and pepper.

4. Once the beans are tender and seasoned, the broth should have thickened. Add more broth or water if it is too thick. The mixture should be soupy but not watery. Discard the bay leaves and thyme. Shred the smoked turkey meat (discarding the bone) and add it to the beans. Serve with white rice.

Buttermilk Mashed Potatoes

Mashed potatoes are America's favorite starch and mine too. When you use buttermilk instead of regular milk or cream, you get a little extra flavor and richness.

Serves 4

WHAT YOU'LL NEED

5 or 6 medium potatoes, peeled, washed, and
    cut into quarters
1 teaspoon kosher salt, plus additional to taste
¼ to ½ cup buttermilk
4 tablespoons unsalted butter, cut into
    small pieces
Freshly ground pepper to taste

WHAT TO DO

1. Place the potatoes in a medium to large pot and add water to cover. Bring to a boil and add 1 teaspoon salt. Reduce the heat for a medium simmer. Cook until the potatoes are fork tender, 20 to 25 minutes.

2. Remove the potatoes from the pot with a slotted spoon and place them in a large bowl. Mash with a handheld potato masher or electric mixer, then slowly work in the buttermilk and butter. Season with salt and pepper to taste. Serve hot.

Mashed Butternut Squash

Butternut squash is versatile. I love to roast them in a sweet way, mash them up, and serve them with steak or risotto. This dish is best in the winter, but you can make it any time of the year.

WHAT YOU'LL NEED

1 large butternut squash, peeled

3 tablespoons unsalted butter

1 tablespoon light brown sugar

$\frac{1}{3}$ teaspoon ground cinnamon

Pinch of freshly grated nutmeg

Kosher salt to taste

$\frac{1}{3}$ cup heavy (whipping) cream

Freshly ground white pepper to taste

WHAT TO DO

1. Preheat the oven to 375 degrees.

2. With a sharp chef's knife, cut the squash in half lengthwise and remove the seeds with a spoon.

3. Place the halves, cut side up, in a baking dish. Add 2 tablespoons of the butter, the brown sugar, spices, and a sprinkle of salt to the halves. Add about ¼ inch water to the bottom of the dish and cover with aluminum foil. Bake until the squash is easily pierced with a knife, 45 to 50 minutes.

4. When the squash is cool enough to handle, cut into smaller chunks and transfer to a mixer bowl. Add the remaining 1 tablespoon butter and the cream and beat until the squash is smooth, about 2 minutes.

5. Season with salt and pepper to taste and serve.

The Bentley of Them All

I have always dreamed big, and ever since I was a child I've wanted the best—not just for me but for my family as well. As a kid I dreamed of a house on a hill with a white picket fence and making enough money so that my mother could stop working two jobs and be financially stable. The kid has never stopped dreaming and striving for the best.

When I became an experienced chef, I decided to move to Las Vegas because that's where some of the most prestigious resorts in the world are. When I arrived in Vegas, I set my eyes on the Bellagio, I called it the "Big B." It was the Bentley of them all. However, not all dreams come without hard work. As a result of my past, getting a job on the strip was very difficult. I got turned down by almost everyone, including the Bellagio, before landing a job at Caesars Palace.

Caesars Palace took a chance on me. They were more interested in my skills and my past experience in the kitchen than in my past transgressions. By this time, I had built a pretty good résumé in the industry. For the next three and a half years, I worked at Caesars Palace, and later the Hard Rock Hotel. Then I started my own catering business, Posh Urban Cuisine. During that time period, I kept trying to get into the Bellagio; I got turned down two more times. Still I wasn't discouraged. I've always worked hard and figured out ways to get what I want, and this time would be no different. The truth is, not many people thought I would get a job in Vegas period, much less at the "Big B." But I didn't allow the dream crushers to discourage me. I continued to develop my image, master my skills, and stay focused.

Almost four years after arriving in Vegas, the window of opportunity finally opened for me at the Bellagio—I got an interview with the big boys. When you're interviewing for a chef position, you have to cook. I was nervous, but deep down inside I knew it was my time to shine. I cooked a seven-course tasting for Executive Chef Wolfgang Von Wieser and his team. He was very impressed with my work and people skills, and he hired me on the spot to run Café Bellagio.

The rest is history, but it was hard work. Many chefs had not survived in the café, and I heard some employees were taking bets on how long I would last. What they didn't know is that I had experience working with some really tough kitchen crews. The Bellagio was my new challenge and I wasn't going anywhere.

At the time the Bellagio had a great crew. I noticed right away that I could learn something from them. They were experienced and, though I was the executive chef, I was still new to this kitchen. I immediately sought out the leaders in the kitchen, praised them for their work ethic, developed relationships with each of them, and asked for assistance during my transition. We worked together, struggled together, and often times shared meals together in the employee cafeteria. I earned their respect. I ran a tight ship, but I was fair and could relate to them. I diffused the kitchen politics, made sure my staff had the best equipment, and cooked on the line every day like everyone else. I never would instruct anyone to do anything I would not do myself.

The café was tough. There were 65 employees and 5 chefs; we averaged 3,500 meals a day. It was nonstop, 24 hours a day, and I was under pressure to maintain food cost, labor cost, and the 5-diamond status held by the Bellagio. There was hardly time to stop and think. We all became instinctive of each other's needs and executed like a high-performance machine. It was intense, but the staff was awesome and they worked harder than most. I recognized them daily and told them how proud I was of their efforts and contributions.

Becoming the first African American executive chef at the Bellagio is one of the proudest moments so far in my life. I love the Bellagio; it's still the Bentley of them all to me.

I was at the Bellagio during key moments in my life. It was there that my literary agent, Michael Palstis, found me, and I began the completion of my memoir that I had started years ago in prison. Though I had been doing motivational talks since my release, it was at the Bellagio that my platform for speaking to at-risk youth and adults about achieving their dreams began to grow. I was still with the Bellagio when I appeared on the *Oprah Winfrey Show* right after the release of my first book, *Cooked*. After the Oprah show, my life became a roller coaster ride. I had to make a hard decision: Stay at Café Bellagio or put all my efforts into the company my wife and I had started some years ago. I tried to do both for a while but it was very difficult. Both the Bellagio and my personal business were very demanding and required an abundance of time. Doing both meant less time with my family, and though I was used to sacrifice and my family was very understanding throughout the years, I just knew that I had to spend more time with them as I pursued the dreams that came to light over the years.

Leaving the Bellagio was very difficult for me. I had no idea what was in store, but as I've said, I always dream big and I don't plan on stopping. The staff at the Bellagio is still like family to me, even today. I go back to visit and think of them often. I drove that Bentley, and I can tell you for sure, the ride was smooth.

At the Bellagio.

DINNERS

When I was growing up, dinner was the most important meal of the day. From fried chicken to crispy tacos to simple sandwiches made with leftovers, we always made a big deal about dinner. Some of these simple recipes are from my childhood. Some are dishes that I perfected over the years in various restaurants where I drew my inspiration from the different cultures of the people I worked with. Most of the side dishes in this book will go well with these dinners.

Friendly Fried Chicken

The great debate over fried chicken always has to do with how best to get that crispy, flavorful outside—oh, and okay, which part of the chicken tastes best fried. Well, these days we know that fried foods are not good for your health, so I recommend you don't eat this dish too often. But every once in a while it's okay to dust off that cast-iron skillet and fry up some good ol' chicken. This was one of the first recipes I learned, thanks to my former mentor in prison, Friendly Womack Jr. What makes it so great is that the chicken gets seasoned *three times,* and the meat is pierced with a fork to let the flavors penetrate. I am not going to say any more. Get your skillet out and follow this recipe to a tee. Oh, and also do this: Fry one wing first to make sure the oil is hot enough and the flavor is what you want before you do the whole batch. Read the story, folks!

Serves 4 to 6

WHAT YOU'LL NEED

¾ cup ground black pepper

⅔ cup kosher salt

3 tablespoons garlic powder

3 tablespoons onion powder

4 tablespoons cayenne pepper

1½ cups all-purpose flour

16 chicken wings

¼ cup buttermilk

5 cups canola oil

WHAT TO DO

1. To make the Friendly spice mix, stir the pepper, salt, garlic powder, onion powder, and cayenne together. Divide it in half and add one-half to the flour. Mix well with a fork and set aside.

2. Rinse the chicken wings and pat dry with paper towels. Place the wings on a flat surface. Using a fork, pierce the chicken wings to allow the spices to penetrate.

3. Tuck the chicken wings at the joint and season them with the second half of the spice mix. Place them in a medium bowl and coat them with the buttermilk. Cover and let marinate in the refrigerator for up to 24 hours.

4. When ready to fry, remove the chicken from refrigerator and dust it well with the seasoned flour. Hit two pieces together to shake off the excess flour.

5. Heat the oil in a 12-inch cast-iron skillet to about 375 degrees. If you don't have a thermometer, test the heat by dipping the end of one wing in the hot oil. If the oil starts boiling heavily, it's too hot. The oil should have a medium boil when the chicken is dropped in.

6. Gently drop the wings in the oil and fry, turning two or three times, until golden brown, 8 to 10 minutes on each side. Remove the chicken from the skillet to a large plate lined with paper towels.

7. Serve with Buttermilk Waffles (page 211) and maple syrup.

WHAT'S THE STORY

Some thirteen years ago Friendly Womack and I had a little chicken business at Club Fed. We sold fried chicken to a select clientele in the yard who would often trade goods and services for it. After Friendly left prison, I ran our business solo. I played with the recipe (which Friendly wouldn't have allowed) and began to marinate the chicken in a little buttermilk. Then I added cayenne to make it a bit spicy. That's the story behind Friendly Fried Chicken. To this day, people love it. When I was executive chef at Café Bellagio, I used this same jailhouse recipe, and it was our number one special next to my braised beef short ribs.

Friendly Womack Jr., former head inmate cook, Red Horse Dining Hall, Nellis Air Force Base, Las Vegas, Nevada

When I met Jeff he reminded me of a younger brother. I started him off in the kitchen making gravy because that was fairly easy. If you messed it up you could do it over pretty quickly. Jeff's a Cancer, and in those days he was an impatient guy. He's changed a lot. He still wants things to move along swiftly, but he's not nearly as impatient as he used to be. I'm really proud of him. He's a master in the kitchen and a good family man. I've even told him that if he made some changes in my fried chicken recipe, they are probably for the best.

My Rigatoni Bolognese

I've taken the basic idea of Italian Bolognese sauce and used ground turkey instead of beef, pork, and veal. By substituting mascarpone for the béchamel, I've also given the sauce a little hint of sweetness. You can serve this sauce with any pasta, or just with a side of cornbread or garlic toast, which is the way I like it.

Serves 4 to 6

WHAT YOU'LL NEED

3 tablespoons extra-virgin olive oil

4 cloves garlic, peeled and finely minced

1 medium onion, peeled and finely chopped

½ green bell pepper, washed, seeded, and
    finely diced

1 pound ground turkey

½ teaspoon dried oregano

¼ teaspoon dried thyme

Kosher salt and freshly ground pepper to taste

2 cups canned crushed tomatoes

¼ cup tomato paste

16 ounces rigatoni or spaghetti

⅓ cup heavy (whipping) cream

½ cup mascarpone cheese

¼ cup finely chopped flat-leaf parsley

¼ cup pitted black olives

WHAT TO DO

1. Heat 2 tablespoons of the oil in a medium to large nonstick pot over medium-high heat. Add the garlic, onion, and bell pepper, and cook until the vegetables are tender, 6 to 8 minutes. Add the ground turkey, oregano, and thyme. Cook, stirring, until the meat is browned, 10 to 12 minutes. Season with salt and pepper. Reduce the heat and simmer, covered, for 15 to 20 minutes.

2. Transfer the meat mixture to a colander to drain, then return it to the pot. Add the tomatoes and tomato paste and stir well. Simmer, covered, for 25 to 30 minutes, stirring every 8 to 10 minutes.

3. Fill a medium pot halfway with water and add 2 pinches of salt and the remaining tablespoon olive oil. Bring to a boil. Add the pasta and cook according to the package directions. Drain well.

4. Add the cream and mascarpone to the sauce, stir well, and simmer for 5 to 6 minutes. Adjust the seasoning with salt and pepper. Stir in the parsley and olives. Spoon the meat sauce into a large bowl and serve with the rigatoni and some bread.

Herb Roasted Cornish Hens

I find Cornish hens a little juicier than regular chicken. You can roast them whole with fresh herbs or split them in half, marinate them, and grill them. Either way they are beautiful on the plate and they have great flavor.

Serves 4

WHAT YOU'LL NEED

4 Cornish hens, washed and cut in half

2 bunches fresh thyme

1½ bunches flat-leaf parsley, washed and
    finely chopped

2 medium carrots, washed, peeled, and
    coarsely chopped

1 large yellow onion, peeled and coarsely
    chopped

2 stalks celery, washed and coarsely chopped

¾ cup extra-virgin olive oil

3 cloves garlic, peeled and finely minced

Grated zest and juice of 1 lemon

Kosher salt and freshly ground pepper to taste

WHAT TO DO

1. Place the hens in a roasting pan. Combine 1 bunch of the thyme, the parsley, carrots, onion, and celery and place it in the cavities of the Cornish hens.

2. Strip the leaves from the remaining bunch of thyme and combine with the olive oil, garlic, and lemon zest and juice. Mix well and rub the herb marinade over the hens. Reserve the excess marinade. Season with salt and pepper. Let the hens marinate in the refrigerator for up to 24 hours.

3. Preheat the oven to 350 degrees.

4. Drizzle the excess oil marinade into a sauté pan and heat over medium heat. Add 2 hens at time and sear on all sides to brown. Place the hens in the same roasting pan and roast for 50 to 60 minutes. Test for doneness by cutting open a piece of hen, usually the thigh. It should not be pink.

5. Let the hens rest for 10 to 15 minutes before serving.

Big Mac's Meat Loaf

I've always loved meat loaf, even the kind they served in my school cafeteria when I was a kid. My version uses many of the things I prefer: ground turkey instead of beef, cornbread instead of bread crumbs, and smoky barbecue sauce on top in place of ketchup. Make some Buttermilk Mashed Potatoes (page 148) to go along with this dish.

Serves 6 to 8

WHAT YOU'LL NEED

1½ pounds ground turkey

½ onion, peeled and finely diced

1½ stalks celery, washed and finely diced

½ green bell pepper, washed, seeded, and finely diced

3 cloves garlic, peeled and finely minced

2 large eggs, beaten

1½ cups cornbread, ground in food processor, or
     bread crumbs

⅓ teaspoon cayenne pepper

1 teaspoon chili powder

1 teaspoon dried thyme

1½ teaspoons kosher salt

1 teaspoon freshly ground pepper

½ cup Smoked Molasses Barbecue Sauce (page 42)

¼ cup ketchup

WHAT TO DO

1. Preheat the oven to 325 degrees.

2. Place the ground turkey, onion, celery, bell pepper, garlic, and eggs in a large bowl and gently mix by hand. Add the cornbread crumbs and spices and continue to gently mix until all ingredients are incorporated. Let stand for about 30 minutes. (To test for flavor, bake a small amount of the meat mixture. Taste and adjust the seasonings.)

3. Pack the meat mixture into a 10-inch loaf pan, cover with aluminum foil, and pierce the foil with a fork. Bake for about 40 minutes, then remove the foil and bake until the meat loaf is browned and firm, 15 to 20 minutes longer.

4. Let the meat loaf sit for about 20 minutes.

5. Turn the pan upside down onto a baking sheet lined with parchment paper and remove the pan. Mix the barbecue sauce and ketchup and brush this glaze on top of the meat loaf. Slice and serve.

My Mother's Grilled T-bone Steaks

You can't go wrong with a T-bone, the porterhouse's little brother, especially since this is now a fairly inexpensive cut. The method I prefer is to brown the steak first and then finish it in the oven with onions on top. You'll discover that's the way to get the best flavor and the juiciest meat. That's the way my mother used to do it.

Serves 4 to 6

WHAT YOU'LL NEED

4 pounds T-bone steaks, approximately
    3 inches thick
2 tablespoons kosher salt
2 tablespoons freshly ground pepper
1 tablespoon Lawry's seasoning salt
2 teaspoons garlic powder
⅓ cup canola oil
1 large yellow onion, peeled and
    thinly sliced

WHAT TO DO

1. Let the steaks warm to room temperature. Preheat the oven to 375 degrees.

2. Mix the seasonings together in a small bowl and sprinkle over both sides of the steaks.

3. Heat a large sauté pan over medium-high heat and add 3 tablespoons of the oil. Add one-quarter of the onion and sauté for 3 to 5 minutes. Place 2 or 3 steaks in the pan and brown on both sides for 2 to 3 minutes. Remove the steaks and place in a baking pan. Add the cooked onion on top of the steaks and bake in the oven for 15 to 20 minutes. Repeat the procedure with the remaining oil, onion, and steaks.

4. Transfer the steaks to a platter and let rest for 5 minutes before serving. Serve on the bone with A-1 steak sauce, our family favorite.

Roasted Cedar Plank Salmon

Many fish markets and fine food shops now sell cedar wood planks for roasting salmon. All you need to do is follow the instructions for soaking the plank before you roast the fish. Make sure the wood is untreated. The cedar gives the fish a wonderful flavor, and it fills the house with a beautiful aroma.

Serves 4 to 6

WHAT YOU'LL NEED

1 untreated cedar plank

4 6-ounce salmon fillets, skin removed

Juice of 2 lemons

¼ cup Spicy Cilantro Pesto (page 41)

8 sprigs fresh thyme

Kosher salt and freshly ground pepper
      to taste

WHAT TO DO

1. Soak the cedar plank in cold water for 2 hours; it should be completely immersed in the water, so weigh it down (a heavy bowl works well). Remove from the water and let sit for 1 hour.

2. Preheat the oven to 375 degrees. Place the cedar plank over your largest stove burner and turn the heat to high. Heat, turning the plank with a pair of tongs, until it begins to smoke and release fragrance, 2 to 3 minutes. Place the plank on a baking sheet.

3. Place the salmon fillets on the plank. Drizzle with the lemon juice and brush with some of the cilantro pesto. Add 2 thyme sprigs to each fish fillet and sprinkle with a little salt and pepper.

4. Bake for 10 to 15 minutes. The cooking time will vary depending on the thickness of the salmon. The salmon should be a little pink in the center. You can serve the salmon on the cedar plank, but it will continue to cook on the hot wood. Remove the thyme and brush a little cilantro pesto on the finished salmon for a more intense flavor.

Sautéed Striped Sea Bass

Here are two simple rules: Don't be afraid of fish and get to know striped bass, a favorite of mine. It's easily available and can be ready in 10 to 15 minutes. It works well with a variety of sauces and condiments. I like to eat this fish with a little caramelized cabbage, sautéed potatoes, and just a little extra-virgin olive oil drizzled on it. Be sure to score the skin before you cook it, so it doesn't curl up.

Serves 4

WHAT YOU'LL NEED

3 tablespoons canola oil

4 6-ounce striped sea bass fillets, scored

Kosher salt and freshly ground white pepper to taste

Caramelized Cabbage (page 128)

2 tablespoons extra-virgin olive oil

WHAT TO DO

1. Preheat the oven to 375 degrees.

2. Heat the canola oil in a nonstick sauté pan over medium-high heat until it's very hot but not smoking. Season the bass on both sides with salt and pepper and place, skin side down, in the sauté pan. Cook until the skin is nice and crispy, 4 to 6 minutes.

3. Turn the fillets over with a spatula and bake until the fish is nice and tender, 4 to 6 minutes. Remove the fish from the oven.

4. Place a spoonful of caramelized cabbage in the center of each dinner plate, then arrange a bass fillet on top. Drizzle the fish with a little olive oil and serve immediately.

WHAT'S THE STORY

Now I surely didn't grow up eating striped sea bass. We had red snapper, whiting, cat-fish, and frozen battered codfish and chips at home. I encountered more exotic (and expensive) fish and seafood at Gadsby's, the Hotel Bel-Air, and the Bellagio in Las Vegas, where world-renowned chefs served them in a variety of preparations. I quietly studied up, and my knowledge of seafood became more extensive. That's the power of books if you use them right.

Cornbread-Crusted Lamb Chops

Every restaurant that I've worked in has offered lamb chops prepared in a variety of ways. For this recipe, I wanted to do a variation on the classic herb-crusted rack of lamb that would make it a little more urban. Instead of crusting the lamb with herbed panko or regular bread crumbs in the customary manner, I added fresh herbs to leftover cornbread and crusted my lamb with that mixture. Get the folks in the meat section to clean the racks for you. I like to serve it with a couple of Southern side dishes.

Serves 4

WHAT YOU'LL NEED

2 racks of lamb, cleaned

2 tablespoons extra-virgin olive oil

5 cloves garlic, peeled and finely minced

5 or 6 sprigs fresh rosemary, stems removed,
   leaves finely chopped

Kosher salt and freshly ground pepper to taste

2 tablespoons canola oil

1½ cups Cakelike Cornbread crumbs (page 199)

3 tablespoons finely chopped flat-leaf parsley

½ cup Dijon mustard

WHAT TO DO

1. Preheat the oven to 350 degrees.

2. Rub the back cap of both racks of lamb with the olive oil, garlic, half the rosemary, and salt and pepper to taste.

3. Heat the canola oil in a large sauté pan over medium-high heat. Using a pair of tongs, place the lamb, cap side down, in the hot pan. Sear for 4 to 6 minutes on all sides.

4. Remove the lamb to a wire rack and let rest for 15 minutes.

5. Combine the cornbread crumbs, remaining rosemary, and the parsley in a medium bowl. Brush each rack lightly with Dijon mustard and pack the cornbread mixture on the back cap of the lamb. Place the lamb on a wire rack on a baking sheet.

6. Roast the lamb for 18 to 20 minutes for medium-rare to medium. Roast an additional 8 to 10 minutes for well-done (cover the exposed bones with foil so they don't burn), but lamb is best served medium-rare to medium.

7. Remove the lamb from the oven and let rest for 5 to 8 minutes. Cut the racks into chops with a sharp chef's knife and serve immediately.

Ground Beef Tacos

Mexican food is a California staple. My take on the taco is a version my sister and I cooked regularly at home and is very different from the traditional taco. I add green bell pepper to my ground beef and sauce the tacos with ketchup. Like most recipes, it can be changed to suit your taste. My tacos are simple and quick to make. They go great with refried beans and a side of sliced avocados.

Serves 4 to 6

WHAT YOU'LL NEED

4 tablespoons canola oil

⅓ cup finely diced yellow onion

⅓ cup finely diced green bell pepper

2 tablespoons finely minced garlic

1 jalapeño pepper, seeded and finely minced

1 pound ground beef

4 sprigs fresh cilantro, stems removed, leaves finely chopped

1 teaspoon chili powder

Kosher salt and freshly ground pepper to taste

12 to 18 corn tortillas or hard taco shells

¼ head iceberg lettuce, washed and thinly shredded

2 cups shredded Cheddar cheese

2 tomatoes, washed, cored, and finely diced

Ketchup or salsa

1. Heat 2 tablespoons of the oil in a medium to large sauté pan over medium-high heat. Add the onion, bell pepper, garlic, and jalapeño and cook until the vegetables are tender, 5 to 6 minutes.

2. Add the ground beef and cook, stirring, until the meat is cooked through.

3. Drain the meat mixture in a colander and return it to the sauté pan. Add the cilantro and season with the chili powder, salt, and pepper. Cook over low heat for 12 to 15 minutes. Remove from the heat and set aside.

4. For soft tacos, heat the remaining 2 tablespoons oil in a medium sauté pan over medium heat. Place 1 corn tortilla in the pan and cook on both sides for about 1 minute. Remove and place it on a small platter lined with paper towels. Repeat with the remaining tortillas. For hard tacos, heat the taco shells in a preheated 250-degree oven until hot.

5. Add the meat mixture, shredded lettuce, cheese, and tomatoes to the tortillas or taco shells. Drizzle ketchup or salsa on top and serve.

Molasses Braised Beef Short Ribs

Several years ago I ate the best slow-braised short ribs I'd ever had at Craft Steak in Las Vegas's MGM Grand. I knew that I made pretty good braised short ribs at Café Bellagio, but after the Craft experience I wanted to improve my version. I went back to our little prep kitchen with my sous chef, Jamie Mendoza, and played around with my recipe. We brought in some different cuts and eventually I told him, let's add some molasses and try marinating the meat before braising it. The result was a hit—one of the best sellers on the menu. Here is the home version. Plan ahead. This is one of those dishes that tastes better the next day.

Serves 4 to 6

WHAT YOU'LL NEED

⅓ cup canola oil

4 to 6 pounds beef short ribs, trimmed and
    cut in half or in 1-bone pieces

Kosher salt and ground black pepper

¾ cup inexpensive dry red wine

3 tablespoons extra-virgin olive oil

1 large yellow onion, peeled and coarsely chopped

1 large head garlic, peeled and coarsely chopped

3 small carrots, washed and coarsely chopped

3 medium stalks celery, washed and coarsely
    chopped

2 bunches fresh thyme

1 bunch fresh rosemary

2 tablespoons whole black peppercorns

6 to 7 cups low-sodium beef broth or Veal Stock
    (page 7)

4 cups canned diced tomatoes

1 6-ounce can tomato paste

4 bay leaves

1½ cups dark molasses

WHAT TO DO

1. Heat half the canola oil in a large sauté pan over medium-high heat. Season half the ribs with salt and pepper and sear on all sides in the oil. Remove the ribs from pan and set aside. Repeat with the remaining oil and ribs. Add the wine to the hot pan and simmer for 3 to 5 minutes. Remove from the heat.

2. Heat the olive oil in a separate large sauté pan over medium-high heat. Add the onion, garlic, carrots, celery, fresh thyme, rosemary, and black peppercorns. Cook until the vegetables are softened, 10 to 12 minutes.

3. Place the short ribs and vegetables in a large slow cooker. Add the red wine and beef broth to cover the ribs by 2 inches. Add the tomatoes, tomato paste, and bay leaves. Bring the mixture to a simmer and reduce the heat to medium-low. Add half of the molasses, cover, and cook for 3 hours. Remove the lid and skim the excess fat from the top. Season with salt and pepper and add the remaining molasses to taste. Continue to slow-cook until the ribs are fork tender, 3 to 4 hours.

4. Transfer the ribs to a plate, discard the vegetables, and strain the cooking liquid into a medium pot. Bring to a simmer, skimming off the excess fat. Let the liquid reduce slightly by boiling it for 15 to 20 minutes. Add the short ribs to the braising liquid and simmer just long enough to reheat the ribs. Serve family style with Buttermilk Mashed Potatoes (page 148).

WHAT'S THE STORY

Chef Jamie Mendoza was my other half at Café Bellagio—a passionate cook who had been a chef at Olives, another great Bellagio restaurant. I truly could not have refined some of the recipes in this cookbook without his help and that of my entire crew at the café. I had confidence in all of you. You are the unsung heroes that make the Bellagio the brand it is today. Thanks for your passion and support. I will never forget you.

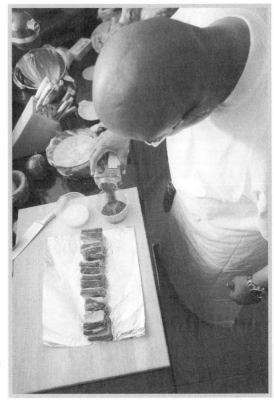

Seasoning and slow-cooking the short ribs is the key to the meat falling off the bones.

Roasted Turkey Drumsticks

My sister ran the kitchen in our little apartment when we were growing up even though my mother, who was the breadwinner, dictated what we would have for dinner. My mother taught my sister how to make our favorite roasted turkey drumsticks. These are great and go with any sides.

Serves 4 to 6

WHAT YOU'LL NEED

4 medium turkey drumsticks

Kosher salt and freshly ground pepper to taste

2 carrots, washed, peeled, and coarsely
    chopped

1 stalk celery, washed and coarsely chopped

½ cup coarsely chopped yellow onion

2 tablespoons extra-virgin olive oil

4 cloves garlic, peeled and coarsely chopped

1 tablespoon freshly ground pepper

8 sprigs fresh thyme, stems removed, leaves
    finely chopped

2 bay leaves

4 tablespoons unsalted butter, thinly sliced

½ cup water

WHAT TO DO

1. Preheat the oven to 350 degrees.
2. Season the turkey legs with salt and pepper.
3. Toss the carrots, celery, and onion with olive oil, garlic, pepper, thyme, and bay leaves.

Spread the vegetables in a large baking dish or roasting pan lined with foil. Spread the sliced butter and pour the water over the vegetables. Arrange the turkey legs on top.

4. Cover the baking dish with aluminum foil and place in the oven. Roast, turning the legs and vegetables every 30 minutes, until the meat is fork tender, 2 to 2 ½ hours.

5. Remove the pan from the oven and let rest for about 20 minutes. Remove the bay leaves and serve the turkey legs with the roasted vegetables and a starch.

Gary Clauson, former executive chef, Hotel Bel-Air, Los Angeles

Robert Gadsby introduced me to Jeff when he was looking for a job in a top hotel. I took a look at him and could tell he was going to make it. He was just that passionate about food.

Jeff was willing to do whatever it took to learn; he never just went through the motions. Some of the other cooks gave him a hard time at first, and Jeff did make mistakes but he never made the same mistake twice.

He started off at the grill station, but he wasn't content with that. He wanted to learn more, so he came in on his days off to learn the sauce station. He came in before his shifts and after his shifts too. Eventually I promoted him to banquet chef, where he was in charge of some of the most prestigious events in Los Angeles.

Jeff is methodical. If he doesn't know something, he will ask. If he can't find out by asking, he will figure out what he has to do. These are the ingredients that have made him successful.

TIME TO GRILL

Grilling in the backyard is a great way to bring your family and friends together without all the formality of sitting around a table and minding your manners. That's part of the fun. But there's also something special about the aromatic smoke coming from the grill, something that takes you back to when families gathered in a local park or in someone's yard for big cookouts.

As a chef, I particularly enjoy the backyard debates about the best way to grill this or that. In the professional kitchen there are no debates—the chef is the man. Not so in the backyard. I also enjoy cooking a few special items for my mother, who has to have her steak cooked a certain way. As long as I do that and supply her with the A-1 sauce she loves, there are no issues from her. When it comes to my children, I set aside one part of the grill for their vegetables and soy burgers. Meat gets cooked on the other part.

There is no one method of grilling. My granddaddy used a huge oil barrel cut in half and turned into a barbecue grill. It even had wheels on it and a smokestack and trays on the sides to hold the meat. I don't think Granddaddy would have approved of the new stainless steel grills fueled by propane gas and equipped with more gadgets than your kitchen stove. But those grills are convenient for the home cook since they make controlling the heat really easy. I have one myself, but I also have an old-school version like my granddaddy's. I call it my "Cadillac Grill." At the end of the day the point is to relax, enjoy family and friends, and eat some good food.

Bone-in Rib-eye Steak

This is one of my favorite steaks. I came to love it after preparing it in many great restaurants. The best part is the meat on the bone because that's where the flavor comes from. This steak is great grilled. I love to rub it with a little bit of Heinz 57 steak sauce or A-1 to give it that back-in-the-day flavor.

Serves 4 to 6

WHAT YOU'LL NEED

1 cup sliced red onion

1 bunch fresh cilantro, stems removed,
    leaves finely chopped

4 cloves garlic, peeled and finely minced

1 tablespoon whole black peppercorns

⅓ cup dry red wine

¼ cup extra-virgin olive oil

Kosher salt to taste

5 bone-in rib-eye steaks, 12 to 14 ounces each

Freshly ground pepper

WHAT TO DO

1. Thoroughly mix together the onion, cilantro, garlic, peppercorns, red wine, and olive oil in a small bowl with a whisk or fork. Add salt to taste.

2. Lay out the steaks and pierce each one several times with a fork to allow the marinade to penetrate the meat.

3. Place the steaks in a large bowl and drizzle the marinade over the meat. Cover tightly with plastic wrap and refrigerate for 4 to 6 hours.

4. Preheat the grill.

5. Remove the steaks from the marinade, letting the excess oil drain off. Place the steaks directly over medium heat, season with additional salt and pepper, and cook to the desired doneness. (Make sure the excess oil has drained off the meat, so the grill flames don't flare up.) For medium, grill the steaks, turning them every few minutes, for 18 to 20 minutes.

6. Let the steaks rest for 3 to 5 minutes, then serve with your favorite backyard side dishes and A-1 or Heinz 57 steak sauce.

Homeboy Skirt Steak

Grilled skirt steaks are your best choice for filling tacos and wraps. I call them "homeboy steaks" because in most kitchens I've worked in, the chef would give the line cooks a slab of skirt steak for their meals after service. The Latinos I worked with would marinate the meat in cilantro, lime juice, olive oil, and other spices according to a recipe from back home. After we finished work, we'd just grill that meat, fill our wraps and tacos with it, add some cheese, and step outside the kitchen to eat.

Serves 4 to 6

WHAT YOU'LL NEED

⅓ cup extra-virgin olive oil

Juice from 2 limes

5 cloves garlic, peeled and finely minced

¼ rod onion, peeled and thinly sliced

2 bunches cilantro, stems removed, leaves
finely chopped

2 jalapeño peppers, seeded and finely minced

2 pounds skirt steaks

Kosher salt to taste

WHAT TO DO

1. Whisk the oil, lime juice, garlic, onion, cilantro, and jalapeño together in a medium bowl.

2. Add the steaks to the bowl and rub the marinade all over them, leaving no part of the meat uncoated.

3. Cover with plastic wrap and refrigerate for up to 3 hours. Remove the steaks from the marinade and let the excess oil drain off.

4. Preheat the grill.

5. Place the meat directly over medium heat and grill, turning every few minutes, for 10 to 12 minutes. Season with salt to taste.

6. Remove the steaks from the grill and let rest for about 5 minutes. Thinly slice, stuff into corn or flour tortillas, and top off with Beefsteak Tomato Salsa (page 52) and some sliced avocado.

Marinated Lamb T-bones

These petite lamb T-bones, officially called *loin chops*, are great for grilling and passing around as an appetizer. They are so tiny you can eat three or four by yourself. My first experience with this cut was at the Hotel Bel-Air when I was the banquet chef. I loved serving and eating them with Eggplant Caviar (page 53). People thought they were unique.

Serves 4 to 6

WHAT YOU'LL NEED

⅓ cup extra-virgin olive oil

2 tablespoons balsamic vinegar

1 teaspoon Dijon mustard

¼ cup finely diced red onion

1 tablespoon minced garlic

2 teaspoons finely chopped fresh thyme leaves

1 tablespoon finely chopped fresh rosemary leaves

Kosher salt to taste

¾ teaspoon freshly ground pepper, plus additional to taste

15 small lamb loin chops

WHAT TO DO

1. Combine the oil, vinegar, mustard, onion, garlic, thyme, rosemary, salt, and pepper in a medium to large bowl and mix thoroughly with a whisk or fork.

2. Pierce the lamb steaks with a fork to allow the marinade to penetrate. Add the lamb to the bowl and toss to coat the meat with the marinade. Cover with plastic wrap and refrigerate for up to 8 hours.

3. Preheat the grill.

4. Remove the lamb from the bowl and let the excess oil drip off. Place the meat directly over medium heat and grill, turning every 3 to 4 minutes, until medium done, 12 to 15 minutes—there should be just a slight hint of pink when you slice one. (Make sure the excess oil has drained off the meat, so the grill flames don't flare up.)

5. Remove the meat from the grill and let it rest for about 5 minutes before serving with your favorite backyard side dishes. I recommend my Eggplant Caviar (page 53).

Finely chopped fresh parsley, rosemary, and thyme
offer the best aromatics.

Grilled Garlic-Herb Chicken

You just can't go wrong with grilled marinated chicken. It's a must-have at any barbecue. I love this recipe because it is the basis for many other styles of preparing chicken on the grill. You can change it up by brushing the chicken with barbecue sauce, curry oil, or even a honey-mustard glaze. A great tomato salad goes well with this chicken.

Serves 4 to 6

WHAT YOU'LL NEED

2 whole chickens

1½ cups Garlic-Herb Marinade (page 49)

Kosher salt and freshly ground pepper to taste

WHAT TO DO

1. Rinse the chickens well and pat dry. Cut the chickens into quarters.

2. Thoroughly rub the chickens with the marinade in a large bowl. Cover and refrigerate for 3 to 5 hours.

3. Preheat the grill.

4. Remove the chickens from the bowl, letting the excess oil drip off. Place the chickens on the grill over indirect heat. Grill, turning the pieces every 5 to 7 minutes, until the chicken is cooked through, 20 to 25 minutes. Test for doneness by cutting open a piece; you should see no pink.

5. Serve with bread and grilled corn on the cob.

Grilled Lobster Tails

This grilled lobster recipe is definitely worth the investment in the price of lobster. Micro manage the grilling process—you don't want to overcook the tails. Butter and lemon juice are great to brush on the tender meat, but don't be afraid to dip these tails in a little of my Smoked Molasses Barbecue Sauce (page 42) afterward.

Serves 4 to 6

WHAT YOU'LL NEED

5 frozen lobster tails

⅓ cup extra-virgin olive oil

Kosher salt and freshly ground pepper to taste

8 tablespoons (1 stick) unsalted butter, melted

2 sprigs cilantro, stems removed, leaves finely chopped

Juice of 2 limes

WHAT TO DO

1. Thaw the lobster tails by running under warm water. Rinse the tails well, removing all impurities. Press each tail down flat on a cutting board, and, using a sharp kitchen knife, cut it in half lengthwise. Rinse again.

2. Arrange the tails, cut side up, on a platter and brush with olive oil. Season with salt and pepper.

3. Preheat the grill.

4. Place the tails, meat side down, on the grill over direct heat and cook until grill marks appear. Using a pair of tongs, turn the tails every few minutes. Grill, basting with butter continuously, until the meat is plump, white, and firm, 12 to 15 minutes total. Remove the tails from the grill, rub with butter, and sprinkle with cilantro and lime juice.

Grilled Jumbo Shrimp

Grilled shrimp is simple to make, and it's one of those backyard dishes that you can serve with almost anything. Be sure to make more than you think you'll need because your guests will be back for seconds and you'll be at the grill for most of the evening.

Serves 6 to 8

WHAT YOU'LL NEED

3 tablespoons extra-virgin olive oil

3 tablespoons finely minced garlic

Juice of 1 lemon

2 dashes Tabasco sauce

2 tablespoons finely chopped flat-leaf parsley

½ teaspoon cayenne pepper

Kosher salt and freshly ground pepper to taste

2 pounds jumbo shrimp, peeled, deveined, and butterflied

½ cup Smoked Molasses Barbecue Sauce (page 42)

WHAT TO DO

1. Preheat the grill.

2. Mix the oil, garlic, lemon juice, Tabasco, parsley, cayenne, salt, and pepper in a medium bowl. Stir well with a fork.

3. Lightly brush the shrimp with the garlic mixture.

4. Place the shrimp on the grill over direct heat. Cook, turning the shrimp every 2 to 3 minutes, until they are plump, white, and firm but still moist, 8 to 12 minutes.

5. Remove the shrimp from the grill and place on a large platter. Serve with a ramekin of barbecue sauce for dipping.

Grilled Corn on the Cob

Grilled corn on the cob is the best corn dish next to creamed corn. This version with Parmesan cheese butter is to die for. Grill enough for everybody to have at least two ears.

Serves 4 to 8

WHAT YOU'LL NEED

8 tablespoons (1 stick) unsalted butter,
    softened

2 sprigs cilantro, stems removed, leaves
    finely chopped

⅓ cup freshly grated Parmesan cheese

Garlic salt to taste

Freshly ground pepper to taste

8 ears fresh corn, shucked

WHAT TO DO

1. Preheat the grill.

2. Place the butter, cilantro, Parmesan, garlic salt, and pepper in a small bowl and mix well with a fork.

3. Brush the corn with the butter mixture, saving some butter for the finished corn. Place the corn on the grill over direct heat and cook, turning the ears every 2 to 4 minutes, until the corn has grill marks and is cooked through, 12 to 15 minutes.

4. Remove the corn from the grill and brush with the remaining butter mixture. Serve immediately with your favorite meat.

Wolfgang Von Wieser, executive chef, Bellagio Hotel, Las Vegas

Jeff is a great guy and a great motivator. He came across really well when I interviewed him. Most people tell you what they think you want to hear. Jeff was impressive to me because he gave us the whole story—the good, the bad, and the ugly. And that's how he got the job. He put together a really nice menu for us, and he worked well with all sorts of people at the Bellagio. Most people get to where they want to go and then forget how they got there. It's all about them. Jeff isn't like that. He respects everyone and never forgets where he came from.

I never realized the impact my culinary journey would have on young people across America. Everyone needs to feel that they have the chance to be successful.

BAKED BREADS AND SWEETS

Baking is in my family's soul. My grandmother Ethel Mae always kept the family cookie jar filled to the brim. When my sister and I visited, we would say hello and then race to the kitchen and grab a handful of chocolate-dipped sugar cookies from the jar. My granddaddy's passion for baking was reflected in his signature box cakes and in his raisin-bread pudding. He loved to offer a slice of either to anyone who walked through the front door. But let me tell you something else: My granddaddy could take a Betty Crocker or generic-brand cake mix and bake the most tender, moist cake you've ever had. His secret was that he added a little pudding to his batter.

When I'm not cooking around the country, I try to bake at home with my wife, Stacy. We usually wait until we have dropped the children off at school and then we get together to bake the children's vegan chocolate chip cookies and our favorite Sunday morning cinnamon rolls with cream cheese icing. Family baking stories are the inspiration behind this chapter, and these recipes are really very simple.

Cakelike Cornbread

The only way I like cornbread is moist and sweet like cake, but you don't often find it made that way. Some folks like to add fresh corn or something spicy and peppery to their batter, but at my house we just like it sweet and light. Try it with maple butter on top. Don't forget to bake it in a cast-iron skillet.

Serves 6 to 8

½ cup cornmeal

1½ cups all-purpose flour

1 tablespoon baking powder

¾ cup sugar

⅛ teaspoon salt

1½ cups milk

2 large eggs

8 tablespoons (1 stick) unsalted butter, melted

Maple Butter (recipe follows)

WHAT TO DO

1. Preheat the oven to 375 degrees.

2. Combine all the dry ingredients in a mixing bowl.

3. Whisk together the milk, eggs, and melted butter in a separate bowl.

4. Without overmixing, slowly pour the egg mixture into the dry ingredients while stirring. Halfway through the mixing process, stop mixing and scrape the bowl, then continue mixing.

5. Pour the batter into a greased 9-inch skillet, baking pan, or muffin tins. Bake until a fork inserted in the center comes out clean, 30 to 35 minutes.

6. Serve with the maple butter.

Maple Butter

You can't go wrong with sweetened butter served on biscuits, waffles, pancakes, or even a slice of toast. Butter rules. But watch the intake as a lot of butter is not good for the heart.

Yields ½ cup

WHAT YOU'LL NEED

8 tablespoons (1 stick) unsalted butter, softened
¼ cup pure maple syrup

WHAT TO DO

Stir the butter and syrup together with a fork in a small bowl. Set aside until ready to use.

WHAT'S THE STORY

Maple syrup and honey were favorites in my home when I was a child. I remember my mother would often bring honey home in a bear-shaped container for my big sister and me. Aside from drizzling the honey on pancakes, we mostly used it in peanut butter sandwiches when we had no jelly.

Dinner Rolls

When I started baking, I was so passionate about bread-making that I actually would stand around to see if I could watch the dough rise. When I make these rolls now, I want each piece of dough to weigh about 3 ounces because that makes a nice-sized dinner roll. Shape the dough the way you like it but make sure you show some love when handling it. This dough can also be made into a great loaf of bread.

Serves 6 to 8

WHAT YOU'LL NEED

5¾ cups all-purpose flour

¼ cup sugar

1½ teaspoons salt

2 packages active dry yeast

1 cup water

1 cup whole milk

8 tablespoons (1 stick) unsalted butter, melted

1 egg, beaten with ¼ cup water

WHAT TO DO

1. Add the flour, sugar, salt, and yeast to the bowl of an electric mixer.

2. Heat the water, milk, and butter in a pan to 120 to 130 degrees.

3. Using the dough hook on low speed, slowly add the liquid to the flour. Let the dough knead for about 3 minutes on medium. Sprinkle a little flour on the side of the bowl to remove the dough from the bowl.

4. Sprinkle a little flour on a work surface and turn the dough out of the bowl. Knead until the dough is smooth and elastic, 10 to 12 minutes. Shape the dough into a round, place it in an oiled bowl, and cover with plastic wrap. Place the bowl in a warm part of the kitchen. Let the dough rise until doubled in size, about 1 hour.

5. Punch the dough down to remove air bubbles. Place the dough on a floured work surface and cut into 3-ounce portions. Shape each portion into a small ball by rolling it on the work surface with the palm of your hand. The top should be smooth. Place the rolls on a greased baking sheet, cover with plastic wrap, and let rise for about 30 minutes.

6. Preheat the oven to 400 degrees. Remove the plastic and brush the rolls with the egg wash. Bake the rolls until golden brown, 15 to 20 minutes. Remove the rolls from the pan and place them on a serving platter.

Wake-up-call Coffeecake

For years I used to eat this coffeecake warm every morning with a brown sugar and nut topping, but you can serve it as a dessert with ice cream. You can also take this basic recipe and improvise by adding berries, bananas, or flavored cream cheese.

Serves 4 to 6

WHAT YOU'LL NEED

2 cups all-purpose flour

1 cup sugar

½ cup (firmly packed) brown sugar

2 teaspoons baking powder

1 teaspoon baking soda

½ teaspoon salt

1 cup buttermilk

8 tablespoons (1 stick) unsalted butter

2 large eggs, beaten

Oatmeal Streusel (page 216)

WHAT TO DO

1. Preheat the oven to 350 degrees. Grease and flour a 13- by 9-inch baking pan.

2. Place all the ingredients except the streusel in a mixer bowl. Mix on low speed until moistened, then beat on medium speed for 2 minutes.

3. Pour the batter into the prepared pan. Sprinkle the streusel over to cover.

4. Bake until a toothpick inserted in the center comes out clean, 30 to 40 minutes. Serve warm or cool.

Black Pepper Biscuits

At my house biscuits are a staple for breakfast, lunch, and sometimes dinner. I often eat buttermilk biscuits split in half and stuffed with meat or cheese like a sandwich. Biscuits, grape jelly, and butter were a favorite of my sister's and mine when we were kids. When we couldn't get them homemade, we baked those really flaky ones that came in a can. Here's a special variation that I make at home for family and friends.

Serves 10 to 12

WHAT YOU'LL NEED

1¾ cups all-purpose flour

1 tablespoon baking powder

½ teaspoon baking soda

½ teaspoon kosher salt

1½ teaspoons freshly ground pepper

⅓ cup unsalted butter, softened

¾ cup buttermilk

WHAT TO DO

1. Preheat the oven to 425 degrees.

2. Sift the flour, baking powder, baking soda, salt, and pepper into a large bowl. Add the butter. Using a pastry blender or two knives, cut in the butter until the mixture resembles coarse cornmeal.

3. Add the buttermilk and stir lightly with a fork. Turn the dough onto a floured surface. Sprinkle a little more flour over the dough if it is sticky. Knead lightly 4 or 5 times.

4. Roll out or pat the dough into an 8-inch circle, about 2 inches thick. Using a 2-inch biscuit or cookie cutter or glass rim dipped in flour, cut the dough into rounds. Gently reroll the scraps and cut into rounds.

5. Place the biscuits on a lightly greased baking sheet, allowing a little space between them. Bake on a lower oven rack until golden brown, 12 to 15 minutes.

WHAT'S THE STORY

Family legend, and let my mother tell it, has it that when I was a baby I could eat a whole can of store-bought biscuits by myself. Well, that's part of the story behind my love of biscuits. Early in my cooking career, Friendly Womack taught me how to bake a biscuit that wasn't heavy and had a little kick to it from the addition of black pepper. You can serve these anytime, and just about anything goes with biscuits.

Sunday Morning Cinnamon Rolls

Almost thirteen years ago when I was learning to bake, a fellow inmate named Royball taught me the secret to making great cinnamon rolls. When working with sweet dough, never overwork it or it will become heavy. I always add a little more sugar and vanilla to this recipe to give it an extra sweet bite. These cinnamon rolls are so good they will make any diet seem unimportant. Oh, and don't forget the glass of ice-cold milk.

Serves 6 to 8

4 cups sifted all-purpose flour

⅓ cup unsalted butter, melted

¼ cup granulated sugar

2 large eggs

Pinch of salt

1 envelope active dry yeast

1 cup milk, warmed to a low simmer (but don't scald)

Cinnamon Roll Filling (recipe follows)

Cream Cheese Icing (recipe follows)

WHAT TO DO

1. Place the flour in a mixer bowl. Whisk the butter, sugar, eggs, and salt together in a medium bowl.

2. Sprinkle the yeast over the warm milk and let stand to dissolve.

3. With the mixer on slow to medium speed, add first the butter mixture and then the yeast mixture in a slow stream. Mix for 2 to 3 minutes, then scrape the bowl and mix for an additional minute. The dough should clean the side of the bowl.

4. Knead the dough on a floured surface until smooth.

5. Place the dough in a lightly greased steel bowl. Cover with plastic wrap and let rise in a warm place in the kitchen until doubled in size, about 1 hour.

6. Punch down the dough on a floured surface and let rest for about 15 minutes. Roll the dough into a rectangle about ¼ inch thick.

7. Make the cinnamon roll filling and spread over the dough. Sprinkle with the nuts. Roll the dough tightly into a log shape. Slice the log 1¾ inches thick and place the rolls in a lightly greased cast-iron skillet or pie plate. Cover and let rise until doubled in size, 30 to 45 minutes.

8. Preheat the oven to 375 degrees.

9. Bake the rolls until golden brown, 20 to 25 minutes. Remove from the oven and let cool down to warm. Make the cream cheese icing and drizzle over the rolls.

Cinnamon Roll Filling

Yields approximately 1 cup

WHAT YOU'LL NEED

1½ cups (packed) brown sugar

2 tablespoons ground cinnamon

1½ teaspoons freshly grated nutmeg

⅓ cup butter, softened

½ cup pecan or walnut pieces

1. Place all the ingredients except the nuts in a mixer bowl and beat until creamy.
2. Spread the filling evenly over the dough and sprinkle with the nuts.

WHAT'S THE STORY

The story behind this recipe goes back to the days when I was away in the mid-1990s. I am very grateful to Mr. Payne and the head baker at Club Fed, Royball, who let me try my hand at making desserts. I became so passionate about this craft that I even considered becoming a pastry chef. I definitely have a sweet tooth, but I keep it under control now.

Cream Cheese Icing

Yields approximately ½ cup

WHAT YOU'LL NEED

¾ cup (1½ sticks) butter, softened
¼ cup cream cheese, softened
1½ cups confectioner's sugar
½ teaspoon pure vanilla extract
Pinch of salt

WHAT TO DO

Beat the butter and cream cheese in a mixer bowl. Gradually beat in the sugar, then mix in the vanilla and salt. The mixture should be creamy. Scrape the bowl and set aside until ready to use.

Buttermilk Waffles

This may sound a little unusual coming from a professional chef but, as a kid, I used to chow down on those frozen Kellogg's Eggo waffles. Remember that commercial "L'Eggo my Eggo?" Well, I thought there was no better waffle in the world than Eggo until I went to Roscoe's Chicken and Waffles in Hollywood. Their waffles are amazing. They're soft and they somehow hold their heat longer than any waffle I'd eaten before. Topped with a scoop of whipped butter and finished with hot maple syrup, they are the waffle to beat. Here's my version . . . combined with fried chicken, of course, just like at Roscoe's. Use the Friendly Fried Chicken recipe (page 157) and lots of maple syrup. Or just have the waffles for breakfast.

Serves 4 to 6

WHAT YOU'LL NEED

1¾ cups all-purpose flour

4 teaspoons sugar

2 teaspoons baking powder

¼ teaspoon baking soda

½ teaspoon ground cinnamon

¼ teaspoon salt

2 cups buttermilk

2 large eggs

½ teaspoon pure vanilla extract

6 tablespoons (¾ stick) unsalted butter,
     melted and slightly cooled

WHAT TO DO

1. Preheat a waffle iron, and if you plan to hold the waffles until serving time, preheat the oven to 200 degrees.

2. Stir the flour, sugar, baking powder, baking soda, cinnamon, and salt together in a large bowl. In another bowl, whisk the buttermilk, eggs, and vanilla until completely blended.

3. Make a well in the dry ingredients and pour in the egg mixture, blending gently until the ingredients are just combined. Add the butter in a slow stream, continuing to blend until the butter is incorporated.

4. Pour a generous ½ cup batter (or more, depending on the size of your waffle iron) into the waffle iron and, using a metal spatula or table knife, spread the batter to within ½ inch of the edge. Close the cover and cook until crisp and golden brown, about 3 minutes. Serve the waffles immediately, or place them in a single layer on racks in the preheated oven while you finish with the remaining batter.

Chocolate-chip Banana Nut Bread

Here's a sweet bread that's quick to make, lasts several days, and freezes well. The nuts give it texture, and the chocolate chips capitalize on that great combination of bananas and chocolate. Don't throw away those brown bananas.

Serves 6 to 8

WHAT YOU'LL NEED

6 ripe bananas

1 teaspoon lemon juice

3¼ cups all-purpose flour

½ teaspoon baking powder

1¼ teaspoons baking soda

1 teaspoon ground cinnamon

½ teaspoon salt

2 cups sugar

2 large eggs

½ cup vegetable oil

1 teaspoon pure vanilla extract

¾ cup chopped pecans

½ cup chocolate chips

WHAT TO DO

1. Preheat the oven to 350 degrees. Prepare two 8-inch loaf pans by spraying them lightly with cooking spray or rubbing with softened butter.

2. Puree the bananas and lemon juice together using a blender or by hand. You should have about 2 cups mashed bananas.

3. Sift the flour, baking powder, baking soda, cinnamon, and salt together into a bowl.

4. Place the banana puree, sugar, eggs, oil, and vanilla in a mixer bowl and mix on medium speed with the paddle attachment until blended. Scrape the bowl as needed. Add the sifted dry ingredients and mix until just combined. Stir in the pecans and chocolate chips.

5. Divide the batter evenly between the loaf pans. Gently tap the filled pans to burst any air bubbles. Bake until the bread springs back when pressed and a toothpick inserted near the center comes out clean, about 55 minutes.

6. Cool the loaves in the pans for a few minutes, then turn the bread onto a cooling rack. Let cool completely before slicing and serving. The bread can be held at room temperature for up to 3 days or frozen for up to 6 weeks.

Granny Smith Apple Muffins

Serves 6 to 8

WHAT YOU'LL NEED

1½ cups all-purpose flour

¾ cup sugar

2 teaspoons baking powder

½ teaspoon salt

½ cup milk

8 tablespoons (1 stick) butter, melted
     and cooled

1 large egg, beaten

Apple Mixture

2 tablespoons butter

¾ cup peeled and diced Granny Smith apple

2 tablespoons light brown sugar

2 pinches freshly grated nutmeg

2 pinches ground cinnamon

¾ cup Oatmeal Streusel (recipe follows)

WHAT TO DO

1. Preheat the oven to 375 degrees.

2. Prepare 2 muffin tins by spraying them lightly with cooking spray or lining the cups with paper liners.

3. Sift the flour, sugar, baking powder, and salt together into a mixing bowl. Make a well in the center of the flour mixture.

4. In a separate bowl, whisk the milk, butter, and egg together. Add the milk mixture to the flour mixture and stir by hand just until the batter is evenly moistened.

5. For the apple mixture, melt the butter in a small sauté pan over medium heat. Add the apple, brown sugar, nutmeg, and cinnamon and cook, stirring, until the apple is tender but not totally soft, 3 to 5 minutes. Transfer to a plate to cool.

6. Fold the apple mixture into the batter.

7. Fill the muffin cups about three-quarters full. Gently tap the filled tins to release any air bubbles. Sprinkle the tops with the streusel. Bake until a toothpick inserted in the center comes out clean, 25 to 30 minutes.

8. These muffins can be served warm or transfer them to a cooling rack before storing in an airtight container.

Oatmeal Streusel

Yields approximately ¾ cup

WHAT YOU'LL NEED

¾ cup all-purpose or cake flour

⅔ cup instant oatmeal

6 tablespoons sugar

1 teaspoon ground cinnamon

½ teaspoon freshly grated nutmeg

¼ teaspoon salt

3 tablespoons unsalted butter, softened

3 tablespoons broken pecan pieces (or your choice of nut)

WHAT TO DO

Combine the flour, oats, sugar, cinnamon, nutmeg, and salt in a mixer bowl. Add the butter and nuts and mix with the paddle attachment until crumbly, about 5 minutes.

Nutty Peanut Butter Cookies

Serves 6 to 8

WHAT YOU'LL NEED

8 tablespoons (1 stick) unsalted butter, softened

¾ cup (firmly packed) brown sugar

¾ cup granulated sugar

¾ cup crunchy peanut butter

2 tablespoons whole milk

1 teaspoon pure vanilla extract

1 large egg

1 ¾ cups all-purpose flour

1 teaspoon baking soda

½ teaspoon salt

WHAT TO DO

1. Preheat the oven to 375 degrees.

2. In a mixer bowl, beat the butter and both sugars until creamy.

3. Add the peanut butter, milk, vanilla, and egg and mix until well blended.

4. Add the flour, baking soda, and salt and mix well.

5. Shape the dough into a log and slice about 2 inches thick. Place the rounds about 2 inches apart on ungreased cookie sheets and flatten the rounds with your fingers. Bake until golden brown, about 12 minutes. Let cool on racks.

Charles Henderson, father

My son loves speaking and he loves cooking. When he's in the kitchen, he's in a different world. I know because I'm a photographer and that's the way I am when I'm taking pictures. When he's speaking, Jeff could talk all day, every day. He knows that to be happy you have to love what you do and he loves both of these things.

I'm not familiar with some of the high-end cooking that Jeff does, but I have good taste buds. When he made some barbecued shrimp with his special scampi sauce and let me taste it, I just lost control. Recently he brought me his gumbo, and I thought it was great. He says he's working on making it even better because he's always trying to top himself. If he brings the new batch by, I might not be able to keep myself away from it.

I'm struck most by how much my son has learned and how fast. He wasn't going to settle for being a fast-food cook. He wanted to do high-end food with the best ingredients. But he also wants to be able to cook for everyone, not just the rich and famous. He hasn't forgotten where he's from.

ICE CREAMS AND SWEETS

For many families, including mine, dessert brings a meal to a joyful close. As kids, my sister and I were drawn to my granddaddy's sugary Southern concoctions and to the baked sweets from the Jewish bakery on Wilshire. On warm days we waited impatiently for the pink-striped Dipsy Doodle trucks that roamed the streets of south central L.A., serving affordable sweets and ice creams to neighborhood children.

There's always a good reason and a good occasion for serving ice cream. I date my love of the frozen treat to the days when I accompanied my granddaddy on the rounds of his janitorial business. He had a contract with 31 Flavors, also known as Baskin-Robbins, and naturally, I loved going to those shops with him. If the owner was around, I usually got to take their little pink spoons and sample my favorites. My grandparents' favorite flavor was "praline and cream," rich with caramel and candied pecans. It must have reminded them of New Orleans. I loved "rocky road" and especially "pink bubble gum," which was only offered in the summer when kids were out of school. That flavor was two treats in one—chewing gum and ice cream. I always saved my gum to chew when the ice cream was all gone. Sometimes if Granddaddy was in a good mood and I had worked hard, he would buy a pint of it for my sister and me.

My love of baking and dessert making has always been a big part of my connection to the kitchen. The recipes in this section reflect that passion and are also ones you will enjoy serving. Each one is a classic made simple for the home cook. My butter pecan ice cream is the all-time greatest. Enjoy a scoop with a little piece of pound cake.

Chocolate S'more Bread Pudding

Any leftover bread will work in this recipe, but if you want to take it right over the top, you have to follow my instructions to the very end. It's the rich chocolate chips, marshmallows, and warm caramel with vanilla bean ice cream on the side that will make you say, "Now that's what I'm talking about!"

Serves 6 to 8

WHAT YOU'LL NEED

3 large eggs

4 cups milk

1 cup sugar

½ cup chopped pecans

1 cup small marshmallows

½ cup small bittersweet chocolate chips

1½ teaspoons ground cinnamon

¾ teaspoon freshly grated nutmeg

1 tablespoon pure vanilla extract

1 teaspoon molasses

⅛ teaspoon salt

3 tablespoons unsalted butter, melted

10 slices pecan-raisin bread

Vanilla Bean Ice Cream (page 239)

WHAT TO DO

1. Whisk the eggs in a large bowl. Add all the other ingredients except the bread and ice cream and stir to combine.

2. Cut the bread into small cubes and fold the bread into the egg mixture. Let stand for 1 hour, making sure the bread is immersed in the liquid.

3. Preheat the oven to 350 degrees.

4. Scrape the bread mixture into a 13- by 9-inch baking dish. Bake until the center is set, about 30 minutes. Serve warm with a scoop of vanilla ice cream

WHAT'S THE STORY

My granddaddy's bread pudding was so good, everyone came over to his house for it, especially my wife, Stacy, when she was craving sweets during her pregnancies. Granddaddy would save the ends of my grandmother's raisin bread and freeze them until he had enough to make a pudding. I never got his recipe, but I came up with one that I think would make him proud. I'm sure he'd have something to say about me adding marshmallows and chocolate chips, but that's Granddaddy!

Pineapple Upside-down Cake

Serves 4

WHAT YOU'LL NEED

½ cup (firmly packed) brown sugar

4 tablespoons unsalted butter, melted

1 16-ounce can pineapple slices, drained

2 large eggs

½ cup granulated sugar

¾ cup all-purpose flour

½ teaspoon baking powder

¼ teaspoon salt

¼ cup pineapple juice

4 maraschino cherries

WHAT TO DO

1. Preheat the oven to 350 degrees.

2. Mix the brown sugar and melted butter and spread evenly over the bottom of an ungreased 8-inch cast-iron skillet or cake pan. Arrange the pineapple slices over the brown sugar mixture and set aside.

3. Beat the eggs together in a mixing bowl. Add the granulated sugar and mix well.

4. Add the flour, baking powder, salt, and pineapple juice and stir until blended. Pour the batter evenly over the pineapple slices.

5. Bake until a toothpick inserted in the center comes out clean, 30 to 35 minutes. Cool in the pan for 15 minutes. Place a cake plate on top of the cake and flip it over onto the plate. Place a maraschino cherry inside each pineapple hole.

Granddaddy's Chocolate Box Cake

I never saw my granddaddy make a cake from scratch except for his Lemon Pound Cake (page 232), but you could not tell that his other cakes came from a mix. They were super moist, probably because he added pudding to the batter. When you don't have time to make a cake from scratch, you can't go wrong with this quick chocolate cake by Betty Crocker.

Serves 4 to 6

WHAT YOU'LL NEED

1 box Betty Crocker SuperMoist Milk Chocolate cake mix

1 cup water

⅓ cup oil

3 large eggs

1 8-ounce can chocolate icing

WHAT TO DO

This one is a bit like cheating, but it's so simple and works so well that even chefs will use it: Follow the directions on the back of the cake box.

Marbled Sweet Potato Cheesecake

My sweet potato cheesecake is a favorite during the holidays. The crust is so good, you can eat it by itself. I always freeze a few cakes for guests. This is so easy, you can even buy pre-baked graham cracker crusts and fill with the cream cheese mixture. You won't go wrong. The recipe was inspired by the great one at Harriet's Cheesecakes in Inglewood, California.

Serves 6 to 8

WHAT YOU'LL NEED

Walnut Graham Cracker Crust (recipe follows)

Sweet Potato Pie Filling (recipe follows)

1½ pounds cream cheese, softened

3 large eggs

¾ cup sugar

2 tablespoons pure vanilla extract

1 teaspoon ground cinnamon

1 teaspoon freshly grated nutmeg

WHAT TO DO

1. Make the graham cracker crust and sweet potato pie filling.

2. Preheat the oven to 325 degrees.

3. Beat the cream cheese in a mixer bowl until smooth. Gradually beat in the eggs and sugar and continue to mix for 2 to 3 minutes.

4. Turn the mixer off and scrape the bowl. Add the vanilla, cinnamon, and nutmeg and beat for 1 to 2 minutes more.

5. To assemble the cheesecake, pour the cream cheese mixture in layers into the crust while adding spoonfuls of the sweet potato pie filling. Take a wooden skewer and crisscross

the cake to create a marbled effect. Place the cheesecake in the oven. On the wire rack under the cheesecake, place a pan filled three-quarters full of water so the cheesecake crust does not double bake. Bake until a toothpick inserted in the center comes out clean, 30 to 45 minutes.

WHAT'S THE STORY

I would put Harriet's Cheesecakes in Inglewood, California, up against the best cheese-cake shops in America anytime. I tried to get a part-time job with Harriet, but she told me her kitchen was family only. That didn't stop me from learning how to make her cakes. I would visit her shop every week to buy a slice. After a month of experimenting, I came up with my marbled version of her famous creation.

Walnut Graham Cracker Crust

This is the best crust. When it's done, it's like a big cookie. It's easy to make but don't let it bake too long. Remember to put a pan of water underneath the cheesecake when you bake it—that way you don't end up baking the crust twice and burning it.

Yields one 9-inch crust

WHAT YOU'LL NEED

1½ cups crushed honey graham crackers

½ cup sugar

½ cup finely chopped walnuts

6 tablespoons unsalted butter, melted

WHAT TO DO

1. Preheat the oven to 350 degrees.

2. Mix the cracker crumbs, sugar, walnuts, and butter on low to medium speed in a mixer bowl.

3. Using your hands, pack the crust firmly over the bottom of a 9-inch springform pan. Bake until the crust starts to bubble up, 12 to 15 minutes. Remove from the oven and set aside to cool.

Sweet Potato Pie Filling

Yields approximately 2 cups

WHAT YOU'LL NEED

2 large sweet potatoes or garnet yams, baked or
    boiled until soft (use 1 8-ounce can sweet potatoes
    if you don't have time to cook them yourself)
2 large eggs, beaten
½ cup (packed) dark brown sugar
¼ cup granulated sugar
2 tablespoons unsalted butter, softened
1½ tablespoons ground cinnamon
1 teaspoon freshly grated nutmeg
⅓ teaspoon salt
½ cup whole milk

WHAT TO DO

1. Peel the sweet potatoes if necessary. Place them in a mixer bowl. Add the eggs, both sugars, the butter, cinnamon, nutmeg, and salt. Using the paddle on medium-low speed, beat for 2 to 3 minutes. Turn the mixer off and scrape the bowl.

2. On medium-low speed, gradually add the milk; continue to beat until the mixture is smooth. Set aside until ready to bake.

Flaky Pie Crust

The crust is what makes my peach and sweet potato pies so special. Make sure you use ice-cold water and don't handle the dough too much after you add the shortening. If you over-work the dough, it won't be flaky.

**Yields two 9-inch crusts or
one double crust**

WHAT YOU'LL NEED

2 cups all-purpose flour
¼ teaspoon ground cinnamon
Pinch of kosher salt
10 tablespoons vegetable shortening
½ cup ice-cold water

WHAT TO DO

1. Mix the flour, cinnamon, and salt in a medium bowl. Using a fork, cut pieces of the shortening into the flour until the mixture looks like crumbs.

2. Drizzle ice-cold water into the flour mixture 2 tablespoons at a time while mixing gently with your hands. Add water just until the dough is moist enough to hold together. Too much water causes the dough to become sticky and tough; too little water causes the edges to tear when it is rolled out.

3. Divide the dough in half and shape each half into a 1½-inch-thick disk. On a lightly floured surface, roll each disk from the center to the edge into an 11-inch circle (or the shape of your baking dish) with a wooden rolling pin.

Peach Cobbler

Peach cobbler is the must-have dessert in our house. There are many kinds of cobblers but peach is king of them all. I have made this recipe as simple as possible.

Serves 4 to 6

WHAT YOU'LL NEED

2 cups reserved peach juice from slicing
  (or canned or bottled juice)
5 tablespoons light brown sugar
¾ cup granulated sugar
1 tablespoon pure vanilla extract
1 tablespoon ground cinnamon
1½ teaspoons freshly grated nutmeg
3 tablespoons cornstarch
3 tablespoons spring water
4 cups sliced canned peaches
1¼ cups (2½ sticks) unsalted butter, sliced
Flaky Pie Crust (page 228)

WHAT TO DO

1. Bring the peach juice to a low simmer in a medium pot. Add both sugars, the vanilla, cinnamon, and nutmeg and whisk until well blended.

2. Whisk the cornstarch and water together in a small bowl, then stir the cornstarch mixture into the peach juice. Simmer, stirring, until thickened, 3 to 5 minutes.

3. Add the peaches and butter to the sauce. Reduce the heat and stir carefully without breaking up the peaches.

4. Preheat the oven to 350 degrees.

5. Prepare the pie crust. Place 1 crust in a 9-inch baking dish. Bake for about 12 minutes. Remove from the oven and let cool for about 10 minutes. Pour in the peach filling and top with the other pie crust. Bake until the crust is golden brown, 30 to 35 minutes. Brush the top of the crust with a little melted butter and sprinkle with sugar. Serve with vanilla bean ice cream.

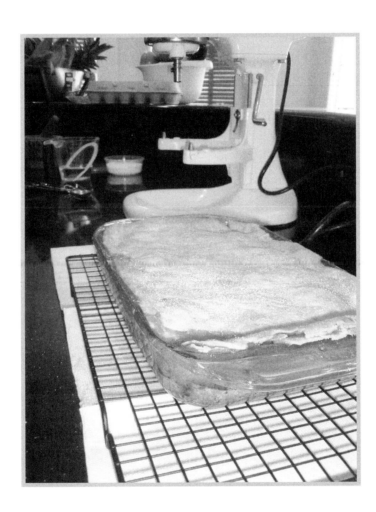

Lemon Pound Cake

This longtime favorite of mine makes a perfect dessert with ice cream and some strawberries. My granddaddy always made his own pound cake. My grandmother liked it best with coffee in the morning. She taught us to "dip and sip," as we say.

Serves 4 to 6

WHAT YOU'LL NEED

1 cup (2 sticks) unsalted butter, softened

1½ ounces cream cheese, softened

½ cup sugar

3 large eggs

1½ cups cake flour

½ teaspoon baking powder

¼ teaspoon baking soda

¼ teaspoon kosher salt

¼ cup buttermilk

2 teaspoons lemon extract

WHAT TO DO

1. Prepare the pan by rubbing with butter and sprinkling with a little flour.

2. Preheat the oven to 350 degrees.

3. Beat the butter, cream cheese, and sugar in a mixer bowl on medium speed until smooth, 2 to 3 minutes. Scrape the sides of the bowl and mix in the eggs one at a time on medium-low speed.

4. Mix the flour, baking powder, baking soda, and salt together thoroughly.

5. Add the flour mixture to the butter mixture and mix on medium-low speed for 1 to 2 minutes. Add the buttermilk and lemon extract and mix until smooth.

6. Pour the cake batter into the prepared pan. Bake until a toothpick inserted in the center comes out clean, 1 to 1½ hours. Don't open the oven the door until the cooking time is up. Let cool for about 20 minutes before cutting. Serve with coffee in the morning or with ice cream in the evening.

Rocky Road Ice Cream

This ice cream goes well without a cone or a piece of cake due to its rich chocolate flavor and the texture of the almonds and mini marshmallows. You can substitute your favorite nut for the almonds.

Serves 4 to 6

WHAT YOU'LL NEED

1 14-ounce can sweetened condensed milk

½ cup unsweetened cocoa powder

3 cups heavy (whipping) cream

1½ tablespoons almond extract

½ cup slivered almonds, toasted

¾ cup miniature marshmallows

WHAT TO DO

1. Mix the condensed milk and cocoa powder in a medium saucepan. Cook, stirring, over low heat until thickened, 5 to 7 minutes. Remove from the heat and stir in the cream and almond extract. Cool quickly in the freezer until chilled.

2. Pour the chocolate mixture into the canister of an ice cream maker and churn until semifrozen. Add the toasted almonds and marshmallows three-quarters of the way through the freezing process.

3. Using a rubber spatula, scrape the soft ice cream into a container and freeze until frozen and ready to serve.

These are three of my favorite ice creams.
It is best to make them ahead of time.

Chocolate Hazelnut Ice Cream

Serves 4 to 6

WHAT YOU'LL NEED

1 14-ounce can sweetened condensed milk

¾ cup unsweetened cocoa powder

3 cups heavy (whipping) cream

1½ tablespoons pure vanilla extract

½ cup hazelnuts

WHAT TO DO

1. Mix the condensed milk and cocoa powder in a medium saucepan. Cook, stirring, over low heat until thickened, 5 to 7 minutes. Remove from the heat and stir in the cream, vanilla, and hazelnuts. Cool quickly in the freezer until chilled.

2. Pour the chocolate mixture into the canister of an ice cream maker and churn until semifrozen.

3. Using a rubber spatula, scrape the soft ice cream into a container and freeze until frozen and ready to serve.

Pink Bubble Gum Ice Cream

This is my favorite childhood ice cream. It's a great treat for children during the warmer months. The best gum to use is Double-Bubble. Cut the gum with a knife and freeze the pieces before adding them to the mix. You can order bubble gum flavoring from specialty candy stores.

Serves 6 to 8

WHAT YOU'LL NEED

¾ cup sugar

3 large eggs

1 tablespoon cornstarch

1½ cups whole milk

1 cup heavy (whipping) cream

1 tablespoon bubble gum flavoring

2 drops pink food coloring

1 cup pink mini gumdrops

WHAT TO DO

1. Beat the sugar and eggs in a mixer bowl until thickened and pale yellow. Beat in the cornstarch.

2. Bring the milk to a simmer in a heavy medium saucepan, then gradually beat the hot milk into the egg mixture. Pour the entire mixture back into the pan and place over low heat. Cook, stirring constantly with a whisk or wooden spoon, until the custard thickens slightly. Be careful not to let the mixture boil or the eggs will scramble.

3. Remove from the heat and pour the hot custard through a strainer into a large bowl. Allow the custard to cool slightly, then stir in the cream, bubble gum flavoring, and food coloring. Cover and refrigerate until cold.

4. Pour the chilled custard into the canister of an ice cream maker and churn until semifrozen. Add the gumdrops as the ice cream firms up a bit. When finished, the ice cream will be soft but ready to eat. For firmer ice cream, transfer to a container and freeze at least 2 hours. Best served in a sugar cone.

Serving ice cream.

Vanilla Bean Ice Cream

America's favorite ice cream, vanilla, goes well with any dessert any day of the year. It's also the base for many other ice creams. It is best made with actual vanilla beans instead of vanilla extract if you want that intense vanilla flavor.

Serves 6 to 8

WHAT YOU'LL NEED

1 cup whole milk

1 vanilla bean, split down the middle

4 large egg yolks

½ cup sugar

1 cup heavy (whipping) cream

WHAT TO DO

1. Pour the milk into a medium saucepan and bring to a boil, then reduce the heat for a low simmer.

2. Place the vanilla bean in the simmering milk and let steep for about 25 minutes.

3. Beat the egg yolks and sugar in a mixer bowl until thick.

4. Carefully remove the vanilla bean from the milk and scrape the seeds into the milk.

5. Pour the milk into the egg yolk mixture and stir. Pour the mixture back into the pan and cook, stirring constantly, over low heat until thickened. *Do not bring to a boil or it will curdle.* When you can see a film form on the back of your spoon, it's time to remove the saucepan from the heat. Let cool.

6. When the custard is cool, stir in the cream.

7. Pour the mixture into the canister of an ice cream maker and churn until semifrozen.

8. Using a rubber spatula, scrape the soft ice cream into a container and freeze for 24 hours.

Butter Pecan Ice Cream

Butter pecan ice cream has been around since I can remember. This ice cream is so good, you don't even need a piece of cake or a sugar cone to go with it. This recipe is also simple to make. You just need an ice cream maker and the ingredients. I advise you to double the recipe. It will disappear quickly.

Serves 6 to 8

WHAT YOU'LL NEED

2 large eggs

3½ tablespoons unsalted butter

⅔ cup (firmly packed) dark brown sugar

½ cup half-and-half

2 cups heavy (whipping) cream

1½ teaspoons pure vanilla extract

⅓ teaspoon almond extract

2 cups pecan pieces

WHAT TO DO

1. Whisk the eggs together in a medium stainless steel bowl.

2. Heat the butter in a medium saucepan over low heat until it begins to brown. Add the sugar and half-and-half. Bring to a simmer and stir well.

3. Slowly pour the warm half-and-half into the egg mixture, stirring constantly with a whisk. Return the mixture to the saucepan over low heat. Continue to whisk until the mixture begins to thicken. Be careful not to let it get too hot or the eggs will curdle. Once it has thickened, remove the custard from the heat and strain it into a bowl. Let cool for 5 to 8 minutes. Whisk in the cream, vanilla, and almond extract and let cool for an additional 20 minutes.

4. Pour the mixture into the canister of an ice cream maker and churn until half frozen. Add the pecans and finish the ice cream.

5. Using a rubber spatula, scrape the ice cream into a container and freeze for at least 8 hours.

Mary Wells Banana Pudding

This classic Southern dessert is among the best—right up there with peach cobbler. This particular recipe was inspired by my late mother-in-law, Motown legend Mary Wells. My wife, Stacy, taught me her mother's secret to making the best banana pudding. "Don't use regular milk; use condensed milk, honey," she told me. And I like to add extra vanilla wafers.

My wife, Stacy, always walks in on me when I'm making her favorite dessert.
"Honey, add more cookies," she'll say.

Serves 4

1 cup sugar

Pinch of salt

¼ cup all-purpose flour

4 large egg yolks

2½ cups condensed milk

½ teaspoon pure vanilla extract

12 to 18 vanilla wafers

2 to 5 bananas, sliced

Additional vanilla wafers and banana slices for garnish

WHAT TO DO

1. Mix the sugar, salt, and flour in the top of a double boiler. Add the egg yolks and milk and whisk until thoroughly blended. Cook, stirring constantly, over boiling water until thickened, 12 to 15 minutes. Remove from the heat and stir in the vanilla.

2. Spread a thin layer of the pudding over the bottom of a 9 by 9-inch baking dish. Cover with a layer of wafers and follow with a layer of bananas. Continue the layering process, ending with a custard layer. Place in the refrigerator and let chill about 2 hours before serving.

3. Garnish with additional cookies and bananas before serving.

My Children's Favorite Fruit Parfait

Almost any fruit would be great in this dessert. My children just love bananas, all types of berries, cantaloupe, melon, and mango, and we use soy yogurt. These same ingredients can also be pureed with a little orange juice into a smoothie.

Serves 4 to 6

WHAT YOU'LL NEED

2 bananas, peeled and sliced

1 cup sliced strawberries

1 cup diced cantaloupe

1 cup diced honeydew melon

1 mango, peeled, pitted, and diced

2 cups plain soy yogurt or any dairy brand

WHAT TO DO

Layer the fruit and soy yogurt evenly in a parfait glass, cup, or bowl. You can alternate the layers to make a nicer presentation. Serve immediately.

Kitchen Central

I'm not one of those cooks who have to be alone in the kitchen. I enjoy it when my wife and kids are around me when I cook, and they like being there. They can help by stirring or they can watch TV or do homework. As I mentioned before, my wife, Stacy, is a vegetarian and three of my kids—Jeffrey Jr. (10), Noel (8), and Troy (6)—are vegans. (Jamar loves his red meat.) I've been developing vegan versions of my food by using soy cream, soy mayonnaise, and vegetable broth in place of regular cream, mayonnaise, and chicken or beef broth, and the kids can follow what I am doing. They all love bread, so we make a lot of that. Troy likes watching it rise. "The bread is growing, Daddy," she says.

When I'm home, we cook almost every day. When we go out to eat, Stacy is really good at finding places that fit our kids' diets and preferences. She's also good at helping me make the transition from professional chef to home cook by getting me to relax in the kitchen.

I think Troy, also known as "Pickle" because she loves them so much, is the one who is going to follow me into cooking. "Who's your daddy?" we ask her. "Chef Jeff, the bad boy of cuisine," she answers. I think I'll be training her soon.

My dreams never stop. Opening my first restaurant on the
Las Vegas Strip will become the pinnacle of my career.

References and Reading for Students, Cooks, and Chefs

Here are a few of the books that I have learned from over the years. They all have inspired me to cook or helped me get into the mind of a great chef. *Becoming a Chef* was the last book I read before I was released from prison. It explained to me that great cooking is always closely tied to seasonal ingredients, something that has inspired my menus ever since. I bought *The Food Lover's Companion* on my first visit to what is now my favorite bookstore, Cook's Library in Los Angeles. It's a reference work that every student, cook, and chef should have. I haven't listed *Joy of Cooking* below because it is so well known, but it remains the bible for the home cook.

Kitchen Confidential is the story of bad boy chef Anthony Bourdain and his journey through the gritty side of the New York restaurant world. Strap on your apron for a wild ride. *The Seasoning of a Chef* is the story of a tough young New Yorker named Doug Psaltis who cooked his way from his grandfather's Greek diner to what many people say is the best restaurant in America, Thomas Keller's French Laundry in Yountville, California. I should add Thomas Keller's *French Laundry Cookbook* too because, like *L'Atelier of Joel Robuchon,* it continues to teach and inspire me in the kitchen.

Index

L

lamb
    Cornbread-Crusted Lamb Chops,
        172–73
    Marinated Lamb T-bones, 189–90
Lemon Pound Cake, 232–33
lobster, Grilled Lobster Tails, 192

M

Macaroni and Smoked Cheddar Cheese,
    142–43
mangoes, My Children's Favorite Fruit
    Parfait, 244
maple syrup
    Maple Butter, 201
    Sweet Potato Soup, 59–60
Marbled Sweet Potato Cheesecake,
    225–27
marinades
    Bone-in Rib-eye Steak, 185–86
    Garlic-Herb Marinade, 49
    Grilled Garlic-Herb Chicken, 191

marinades *(cont.)*
    Grilled Marinated Turkey and Steak
        Satays, 31–32
    Homeboy Skirt Steak, 187–88
    Marinated Lamb T-bones, 189–90
    Marinated Watermelon Cubes, 16–17
marshmallows
    Chocolate S'more Bread Pudding,
        221–22
    Rocky Road Ice Cream, 234
Mary Wells Banana Pudding, 242–43
mascarpone cheese, My Rigatoni
        Bolognese, 160–61
Mashed Butternut Squash, 150
Mashed Potatoes, Buttermilk, 148
mayonnaise
    Cole Slaw, 46
    Dill Pickle Potato Salad, 83–84
    Honey-Mustard Dressing, 93
    Pastrami Sandwich, 115
    Russian Dressing, 98
    Spicy Tartar Sauce, 45
    White Albacore Tuna Sandwich, 116
Meat Loaf, Big Mac's, 164–65
Mendoza, Jamie, 176, 178
mint
    Marinated Watermelon Cubes, 16–17
    My Children's Favorite Fruit Salad, 82
molasses
    Molasses Braised Beef Short Ribs,
        176–78
    Smoked Molasses Barbecue Sauce, 42
Morton, Peter, 87–88

S

W

Waffles, Buttermilk, 211–12

Wake-up-call Coffeecake, 204

walnuts

Candied Walnuts, 50

Cinnamon Roll Filling, 209–10

Field Greens and Apple Salad, 79–80

Walnut Graham Cracker Crust,
226–27

watermelon

Marinated Watermelon Cubes, 16–17

My Children's Favorite Fruit Salad, 82

West Coast Chopped Salad, 85–86

White Albacore Tuna Sandwich, 116

White Bean Soup and a Sandwich, 65–66

wine

Barbecued Shrimp Scampi, 27–28

Bone-in Rib-eye Steak, 185–86

wine *(cont.)*

Molasses Braised Beef Short Ribs,
176–78

Sweet Potato Risotto, 137–38

Womack, Friendly, Jr., 19, 157, 158, 159

Worcestershire sauce

Buttermilk Dressing, 97

Creamy Blue Cheese Dressing, 91

Y

yams. *see* sweet potatoes/yams

yogurt

Buttermilk Dressing, 97

Creamy Blue Cheese Dressing, 91

My Children's Favorite Fruit Parfait, 244